MOVING BEYOND THE COMFORT ZONE IN PSYCHOTHERAPY

MOVING BEYOND THE COMFORT ZONE IN PSYCHOTHERAPY

Nancy A. Bridges

Jason Aronson
Lanham • Boulder • New York • Toronto • Oxford

Published in the United States of America
by Jason Aronson
An imprint of Rowman & Littlefield Publishers, Inc.

A wholly owned subsidary of
The Rowman & Littlefield Publishing Group, Inc.
4501 Forbes Boulevard, Suite 200, Lanham, Maryland 20706
www.rowmanlittlefield.com

PO Box 317
Oxford
OX2 9RU, UK

British Library Cataloguing in Publication Information Available

Library of Congress Cataloging-in-Publication Data

Bridges, Nancy A.
  Moving beyond the comfort zone in psychotherapy / by Nancy A.
Bridges.
      p. cm.
  Includes bibliographical references and index.
  ISBN 0-7657-0344-0
  1. Psychotherapist and patient. 2. Psychotherapy—Methodology. I. Title.

  RC480.8.B755 2003
  616.89'14—dc21   2002038500

Printed in the United States of America

∞™ The paper used in this publication meets the minimum requirements of
American National Standard for Information Sciences—Permanence of Paper
for Printed Library Materials, ANSI/NISO Z39.48-1992.

To Helen and Walter

The author gratefully acknowledges permission to reprint portions of the following material:

Bridges, N. (1994). Meaning and management of attraction: Neglected aspects of psychotherapy training and practice. *Journal of Psychotherapy* 31: 424–433. Copyright © 1994 *Journal of Psychotherapy*. Portions reprinted with permission in Chapter 3.

Bridges, N. (1999). Psychodynamic perspective on therapeutic boundaries: Creative clinical possibilities. *Journal of Psychotherapy Practice & Research* 8(4): 292–300. Copyright © 1999 *Psychotherapy Practice & Research*. Portions reprinted with permission in Chapters 1, 2, 5.

Bridges, N. (2000). The role of supervision in managing intense affect and constructing boundaries in therapeutic relationships. *Journal of Sex Education and Treatment* 24(4): 218–225. Copyright © 2000 *Journal of Sex Education and Treatment*. Portions reprinted with permission in Chapter 6.

Bridges, N. (2001). Therapist self-disclosure: Expanding the comfort zone. *Journal of Psychotherapy* 38(1): 21–30. Copyright © 2001 *Journal of Psychotherapy*. Portions reprinted with permission in Chapter 4.

"The meeting of two personalities is like the contact of two substances: if there is any reaction, both are transformed."

—Carl Gustov Jung

CONTENTS

ACKNOWLEDGMENTS

I always believed that the relationship was the heart of the matter, and that I was blessed to be mentored for many years by Paul Russell, who along with my patients deepened my understanding of what really helps people heal and grow. I wrote to Paul in his last days and commented that his life's work would live on in consulting rooms across the country. I like to believe that my work is in part a tribute to him.

Many friends and colleagues have offered their time and support, and they played an instrumental role in the writing of this book. Fran Givelber, LICSW, and Chris McElroy, Ph.D., read drafts of every chapter with great care and provided insightful clinical comments and editorial suggestions. Juliet Faithful, LICSW, Anne Fishel, Ph.D., Jeffrey Kerr, LICSW, Charlotte Temins, Ed.D., and Anna Wolff, M.D., read drafts of chapters of the book with sensitivity and thought of ways to improve the manuscript that would never have occurred to me. My peer group, Anne Fishel, Ph.D., Beth Harrington, Ph.D., Chris McElroy, Ph.D., Paula Rauch, M.D., and Sue Wolff, M.D., could always be counted on to provide an honest outside view with respect and compassion. During the last sixteen years, they have been an unfailing source of support, comfort, and professional and personal inspiration.

Over the years the written work of Lou Aron, Ph.D., Jody Davies, Ph.D., Darlene Ehrenberg, Ph.D., Glen Gabbard, M.D., Irwin Hoffman, Ph.D., Karen Maroda, Ph.D., and Stephen Mitchell, Ph.D., has kept me company, provided clinical inspiration, and deeply influenced my evolving practice. Closer to home, there are many luminaries that have profoundly influenced my practice. In the Department of Psychiatry at Cambridge Health Alliance, and Harvard Medical School, my thanks to Jim Beck, M.D., Les Havens, M.D., Nina Masters, LICSW, and Carol Nadelson, M.D., who have over the years supported my clinical teaching, writing, and in some cases been invaluable clinical teachers as well. I feel deeply appreciative and indebted to Judy Herman, M.D., and Anna Wolff, M.D., who have been important clinical teachers and have profoundly affected my work. Thanks to Karlen Lyons-Ruth, Ph.D., who through her research, writing, and our discussion of cases has opened new windows into theories of therapeutic change.

I am indebted to my colleagues, students, and supervisees. Thanks to my students in the Department of Psychiatry at Cambridge Health Alliance and at Smith College School for Social Work. In these courses and with supervisees, I was fortunate to find gifted, engaged students who challenged me to share the details of my clinical work and articulate my beliefs and thinking. In the process my students taught me as much as I offered them. Special thanks to Phoebe Sessions, Ph.D., who took a risk and allowed me to introduce a course on erotic feelings when this course subject was unheard of and taboo. She has remained an unfaltering ally in the discussion and teaching of the taboo.

My deepest gratitude goes to my patients, who continue to teach me about this intimate endeavor and allow me to discover parts of myself anew and again as well. While identities have been concealed, my patients have allowed me with open hearts to use their stories and their words.

To my family, Bill, Ian, and Gabe, heartfelt thanks and all my love, as you are the font of many blessings. Each of you has taught me more about myself than you know and the deep pleasures and challenges of closeness and connection. For your love, companionship, sense of humor, gift for distraction, and above all faith in me, I am deeply appreciative. To my husband, Bill, I am indebted and grateful. A gifted writer and even more talented editor, he has been an invaluable reader, offering significant and subtle suggestions and improving every page he touched. Thanks for granting me time off and doing all the heavy lifting around shepherding the boys into the next leg of their academic journeys. As always, the boys and I are deeply grateful for a job so lovingly and well done.

PREFACE

This is a book about therapeutic intimacy and change. Creating a safe place so that our patients can become deeply engaged with themselves and with us is no small feat. Only if we successfully create safety and a coherent collaborative frame will we be able to identify emotional scar tissue and move to developmental relational edges. How do we create a safe place and allow our patients to use us for developmental relational aims? Deep engagement in the intimate process of knowing and being known and expanding relational knowledge often involves the therapist's comfort and capacity to bear intense affect and move outside her comfort zone. This book is an effort to provide therapists with a cognitive relational latticework that might serve as an anchor and inform their own clinical work so that they might have enough company and courage to move outside their comfort zone to an intimate edge with their patients.

While my work and relationships with patients have been endlessly pleasurable and challenging, for many years I struggled with the specifics of my practice, namely the details of what I say and do with patients. I frequently felt as if I were violating unwritten rules: moving in too close, offering unusual solutions, engaging deeply with patients to build a relational bridge back to hope and healing. For some time I have struggled and searched to identify theoretical constructs that capture what I believe is valuable to patients and facilitative of therapeutic change. With an integration of relational intersubjective theories and developmental research, I have found a theoretical home base. It is my hope that these clinical stories will capture the readers' imagination and be a catalyst for their own journey of articulating what they value and believe is at the heart of deep therapeutic engagement and change.

As a therapist, as long as I can remember, I wished to hear what other therapists said to their patients and I frequently asked them. It was always an awkward moment because in my experience, people tend to describe the moment or the conversation and not give the conversational details. What did you say? What words did you choose? Why that word? What was your tone of voice and energy level? In this book, I have tried to satisfy that longing and curiosity by providing the details of the relational moment and movement both internally and interpersonally in the consulting room. By doing so I hope the clinical narratives and theoretical discussions will be of interest to therapists at varying professional stages. Striving to cover enough theoretical ground so any novice can follow along, I present the details of what I said and did with patients and their words to me. I hope that these clinical narratives will interest experienced clinicians as well.

The clinical examples in the text are from my psychotherapy and consultation practice. In some cases the material has been disguised or represents a composite of case material. In many instances, while I have concealed my patient's identity, I present my work with patients. Even though I have protected confidentiality with concealment, I believe patients have a right to privacy and to refuse the public use of personal stories. Holding this tenet, I requested my patients' permission to use their material and offered to share with them the text. A special thanks goes to patients who allowed me to use excerpts from many sessions. In some cases, patients read the piece in advance and critiqued my account of our work, correcting inaccuracies and enhancing its readability.

1

CREATING A
SAFE PLACE

The pleasure and privilege of being a psychotherapist is accompanied by tremendous responsibility. Our patients come to us in often-unspeakable anguish with compelling personal stories of tragedy, betrayal, and abandonment that shape their views of themselves and their relational world. They hope we will be of help and yet fear this relationship will feel like all the other relationships they have known. As therapists, we too are often fearful of deep engagement because of feelings stimulated in us and because of confusion about what is useful therapeutically.

Psychotherapy, when successful, is a deeply personal and intimate endeavor for both the patient and the therapist. Boundaries in the therapeutic relationship are essential to provide a safe forum for deep emotional engagement with a therapeutic purpose. Creating a safe place for destabilizing affect and the unfolding of the therapeutic relationship opens up the space for emotional engagement between patient and therapist that may lead to transforming affective, self, and relational change. Through the interpersonal relationship with a therapist, a patient may change her internal landscape, altering her sense of herself and her capacity to manage affect and relate in the world. Clarity regarding treatment boundaries allows the therapeutic work to move safely to an intimate affective and relational edge.

The material I present here is based upon my clinical practice and evolving thought on these matters during twenty-three years of clinical and academic work. It has been a process of growth and change informed by new theoretical perspectives, influence from my patients, and advances in my own willingness to take risks. I share with you ideas that have guided my thinking and have been essential to my practice. While these processes and concepts have been profoundly valuable in my work with patients, I believe that each therapist must develop her own clinical voice shaped in part by her values, personal life experiences, temperament, personal treatment, and professional mentors. Establishing an approach to treatment within a theoretical structure that works for you and your patients is an ongoing developmental professional process. I hope the material presented will engage therapists in that process.

Therapists want to know, "How deeply personal should psychotherapy be?" How much of the therapist's self should be visible or present? Is there a place for touch? How self-revealing should one be? Is it ever useful to declare feelings of love, sexual attraction, or anger with a patient? What's harmful, what's useful, and the question of how to chart a sound course through the gray areas of clinical-decision making are challenges for many therapists.

Although in recent years there has been a shift to a more open stance in reporting the therapeutic conversation, a shroud of secrecy surrounds what is actually said and done in the consulting room. Neither therapists nor patients benefit. At conferences, therapists discuss their cases but often focus heavily on the patient. The audience is left to wonder what specifically the therapist said or did. What language was used? What was the tone? Even in the literature, therapists retreat behind descriptive accounts of sessions, particularly during moments of urgency.

As a young therapist, I found myself immersed in a passionate state with a psychotherapy patient, embarrassed and ashamed of my feelings and technically adrift. For guidance, I turned to the literature only to find what I now know was a brave pioneering account by Harold Searles describing cases in which he experienced "a romantic and erotic desire to marry" (1965, p. 284). While groundbreaking at the time, Searles' account hardly captured my affective and subjective experience and left me with no technical assistance about how to proceed with my patient. I worry therapists continue to feel inadequately informed by conferences and the literature about the formulation and technical management of intense feelings in therapeutic relationships. Deep engagement with patients and the feelings evoked present lifelong clinical challenges for clinicians (Bridges 1993, 1994, 1995, 1998, 1999, 2000, 2001; Davies 2002; Gabbard 1989, 1991, 1993, 1994a, 1994b, 1996, 2000; Gabbard and Lester 1995; B. Pizer 2000; S. A. Pizer 2000).

More openness and transparency concerning the therapeutic conversation and process would benefit patients and therapists. In that spirit, I share my work striving to be as open and vulnerable with the reader as my patients have been with me. I present case material from my psychotherapy, consultative, and teaching practice depicting critical moments in the therapeutic relationship. Sharing details of what transpired both within and between participants, I hope to capture the essence of the therapeutic moment and movement. In some instances, case material has been disguised and identifying data about patients altered. In other cases, with my patients' consent, I present material from my psychotherapy and consultation practice, concealing patients' identities.

As a therapist and teacher of psychotherapists, I am invited to consult on other clinicians' cases. Palpable shame and anxiety are evident as therapists' struggle to disclose what they actually said or did with a patient during moments of self-other confusion or affective disequilibrium. Brave, ethically minded therapists proceed through their anxiety, disclosing troubling moments with a trusted mentor or colleague, but it takes courage and is difficult. Therapists worry about being harshly judged as being unhelpful to their patients or as crossing therapeutic boundaries. A desire to protect professional self-esteem and a reluctance to disclose the most troubling therapeutic moments or cases often prevails. The confused therapist and the confusing therapeutic process are often left unattended.

Senior clinicians espouse passionately held contradictory positions, which makes formulating useful interventions a conceptual and clinical minefield for therapists (Bridges 1994; Davies 1994a, 1994b; Fishman 1999; Gabbard 1994a, 1994b; Gutheil and Gabbard 1993; Slavin et al.

1998). The range and diversity of clinical theories and opinions are staggering. If you consult twelve experts regarding a clinical dilemma and formulation, you are likely to receive twelve different expert opinions on how to proceed. A manuscript I presented to an American Psychiatric Association psychotherapy journal for peer review was returned to me with diametrically opposite comments on the same clinical vignette. One reviewer assessed the vignette as a dangerous example that should not appear in print, while the other reviewer felt the vignette was the redeeming feature of an otherwise ordinary manuscript. It is no wonder that therapists are confused about the ethical construction of creative, clinically useful interventions in therapist-patient dyads.

A therapist needs a conceptual and theoretical framework to inform and guide her therapeutic work. A theoretical framework grounds a therapist during times of destabilizing relational repetitions that may be accompanied by intense affect. A cognitive-conceptual frame may be an invaluable tool for keeping one's balance while formulating cross-identifications and relational scenarios that threaten to pull the therapist out of dyadic engagement (Bridges 2000; L. Epstein 1995; Gabbard 2000; B. Pizer 2003). In order for a therapist to develop comfort in her assessment and decision making regarding boundaries and psychotherapeutic work, she needs to begin with a thorough understanding of boundaries from an ethical, intrapsychic, and interpersonal stance. In addition to an understanding of boundaries, a therapist's working knowledge of other guiding concepts is needed. Transference, projective identification, and enactment provide conceptual tools to help contain and formulate moments of self-other boundary confusion and intense affect. Even with a solid theoretical foundation, forums to routinely present her work and access to trustworthy consultants will be invaluable and necessary throughout a therapist's career (Bridges 2000; Gabbard 2000; B. Pizer 2000; S. A. Pizer 2000).

Developing the capacity to formulate a case is a hard-won but critical therapeutic skill. A theoretical structure and theory of therapeutic action both ground the therapist and the treatment process, allowing for fluidity and creativity around essential understandings. The therapeutic process of sorting out mutual transference, enactments, and negotiating unwanted affect is, in fact, the intimate edge where transforming negotiations most often occur (Aron 1991, 1992, 1996; Bridges 2001; Cooper 1998b; Davies 1994a; Ehrenberg 1992, 1995; Hoffman 1983, 1992a, 1992b, 1994; Maroda 1999a, 1999b; McLaughlin 1991, 1995, 1996, 2000). Boundary dilemmas illuminate a patient's most painful and troubling affective and relational scenarios that represent heightened opportunities for shifts in relational knowledge. A relational perspective on boundary dilemmas that focuses therapeutic exploration and promotes the use of these issues to expand affective experience and self-other knowledge is most valuable.

BOUNDARIES

Professional boundaries are the "limits that allow for a safe connection based on the patient's needs" (Peterson 1992, p. 46). The fiduciary principle is the essential concept that establishes the basis for all treatment and treatment relationships. This principle specifies that the therapist will act solely based upon the needs of the patient. Codes of ethics dictate such an ethos of professional care. Privileging the patient's needs creates an essential sacred pact between therapist and patient that is necessary for the development of trust and for therapeutic work to take place. Without a mindful commitment to this principle, a therapist may abuse therapeutic power and use her patients for her own needs, causing enormous suffering and damage. Tragically, therapists from all disciplines have witnessed numerous examples of egregious professional boundary violations committed by colleagues and mentors (Applebaum and Jorgenson 1991; Gabbard 1989, 1993, 1994a; Herman et al. 1987; S. A. Pizer 2000; Strasberger et al. 1991).

TREATMENT FRAME

Psychotherapy requires a frame that delineates the purpose and meaning of the relationship and defines and articulates the work to be done. Clear, consistent, predictable boundaries create a safe place and frame for the treatment relationship. Without a clear frame and consistent boundaries, the treatment relationship will not develop the safety necessary to permit the expression of shameful, unspeakable feelings and experiences that the patient needs to identify and master (R. Epstein 1994; Gabbard and Lester 1995; Hoffman 1983).

Hoffman (1992b) outlines the structure and frame necessary to allow for the symbolic unfolding of affects and issues in the treatment relationship:

> The essential features include a circumscribed time and place; the asymmetry of personal expression with the focus on the patient; a primary interest in exploring the patient's experience, conscious, unconscious, past, and present; and a commitment by the therapist to critical self-reflection of her own participation; and a sense of the relationship as a whole is viewed as a means of promoting the patient's development. (Hoffman 1992b, p. 302)

This conceptualization of the treatment frame focuses on the exploration of the patient's experience to make sense of past experiences and to facilitate affective development and relational growth within an empathic, caring, and concerned relationship.

A therapist who holds a collaborative approach informs her patient, maximizing participation and demystifying the therapeutic process. A collaborative stance protects the patient and the therapeutic process. A well-informed consumer is a great therapeutic asset, not a threat to the process. I believe such a treatment frame and structure creates clarity of purpose and a safe place for emotional engagement and therapeutic work.

TREATMENT BOUNDARIES AND CLINICAL STYLE

"The treatment boundary is a psychological containment field maintained by the therapist's mental capacity to encompass the patient's symptomatology and symbolic communications" (R. Epstein 1994, p. 90). Treatment boundaries provide the built-in structure to contain and process communications (R. Epstein 1994; Gabbard and Lester 1995). Intrapsychic and interpersonal therapeutic boundaries need to be permeable, allowing for mutual influence, and yet offer containment and holding for intense affective experiences (Gabbard and Lester 1995; Ogden 1982, 1985, 1994; Russell 1976a, 1976b, 1983; Stolorow et al. 1997; Tansey and Burke 1989, 1991; Teicholz and Kreigman 1998; Waldinger 1994; Winnicott 1958). Effective therapeutic boundaries that are reasonably secure and permeable paradoxically protect and allow both therapist and patient to cross boundaries psychologically with fantasies and feelings, enriching therapeutic dialogue (Bridges 1999, 2000; Ehrenberg 1992; Gabbard 1995; Gabbard and Lester 1995; Maroda 1991, 1999a, 1999b). Within an ethical framework, each therapist must decide which treatment boundaries suit her personal and clinical style.

A therapist has much freedom to experiment and to discover the clinical style and practice that appeals to her. Her choices will undoubtedly be influenced by many personal as well as professional factors. I believe that personal psychotherapy for future or practicing psychotherapists is essential and will provide one model of treatment. The shaping influences, both positive and negative, of a therapist's personal treatment experience must not be overlooked. Heightened conscious awareness of how this instrumental experience affects her practice will be beneficial. Therapists who were interviewed concerning the therapeutic challenges of treating therapist patients state clearly that they mindfully try to replicate the aspects of their personal therapy and therapeutic relationship that were beneficial to them. They also strive not to replicate the aspects of their personal treatment that they found unhelpful (Bridges 1993).

Personal treatment experiences become conscious and unconscious templates for our own psychotherapy practices. A therapist may begin by reviewing her personal psychotherapy experience. How were interpersonal and treatment boundaries handled in her personal treatment? Was touch included? How close and open was the therapeutic relationship and dialogue? Were sexual and loving feelings and disappointment and anger identified and discussed openly in the therapeutic relationship? How was power handled? Did she feel safe? Was the therapist transparent and visible in the process or were her feelings and thinking revealed indirectly?

I recommend that therapists, as much as humanly possible, consciously take hold of how their personal treatment influences their conduct as a therapist. If important issues and affects were neglected or mishandled in her therapy experience, a therapist may want to study her values and personal style. How would she like to technically and relationally handle these issues with her patients? Colleagues and mentors may be instrumental in facilitating the development of a personally crafted treatment approach that incorporates the best aspects of her treatment legacy and moves beyond what her therapist was able to offer her.

Competent therapists may have very different personal and professional boundary styles and practice approaches. When therapists are choosing a therapist for themselves or loved ones, they not only want a therapist who is competent; often they have very specific requirements regarding relational style and personality. They want to know what it will feel like to sit with therapist *X*. I believe it is essential that a therapist honor the fiduciary contract, be emotionally honest, and be willing to reveal her feelings and thinking. Being open to influence and relying upon her patient's strengths and expertise while taking responsibility for her contribution, both positive and negative, provide the foundation for emotionally honest dialogue. Therapists who usefully share motives, intent, and theory of therapeutic action, personal narratives, and above all affective responses with patients facilitate their patients' self-awareness and affective mastery. To be unwilling to ever do so truncates the therapeutic relationship and conversation and stifles developmental possibilities.

The range and diversity of possible clinical styles should not be confused with competent ethical care. Practice styles that violate boundaries and use patients for the therapist's own purposes are harmful. Practice styles in which therapists are emotionally and relationally unavailable and absent are also harmful. Treatment and interpersonal boundaries exist on a continuum and are co-constructed by the needs of each therapeutic dyad. Competent care of patients requires that the therapist inquire: "Whose needs will this meet?" "What is the therapeutic motive and rationale for this intervention with this particular patient?" "What will I gain therapeutically and what will I lose with this intervention?" "Where am I hoping the therapeutic process and relationship will move to with this intervention?" Often we simply don't know the answer to these questions in advance, and most often the formulation of the moment occurs after the intervention. Nevertheless, I believe it is important to anticipate as best as we can untoward sequelae while remaining open to novel outcomes.

Mitchell (2000) advises therapists that neither expressiveness nor restraint in themselves are useful guides to the formulation and management of intense feelings; both positions may be helpful or injurious to the therapeutic process. Rather, the "central feature of the craft is to struggle with these distinctions, to make what seem to be the best choices at the time, and continually to reconsider past judgments and their sequelae, in order to expand and enrich the context in which current choices are made" (Mitchell 2000, p. 146). Juggling the tension and benefit between spontaneity and restraint while remaining the guardian of the therapeutic process opens up space for creative and deep engagement with our patients.

TRANSFERENCE

Theoretical shifts that conceptualize the therapeutic relationship as dyadic and relational in nature emphasize the mutual bidirectional interactive influence between therapist and patient in the development of the transference (Aron 1991, 1992, 1996; Bollas 1987; Bromberg 1991, 1998; Foreman 1996; Fosshage 1994, 2000; Hoffman 1992a, 1992b, 1994; McLaughlin 2000; Mitchell 1988). In a relational model, transference refers "to the primary organizing affective and relational patterns or schemas with which the therapist and patient construct and assimilate his or her experience of the treatment relationship" (Fosshage 1994, p. 271). Our best window into these relational scenarios is to focus on "what a person does with and to other people in both fixed and unpredictable relational patterns" (Bromberg 1998, p. 310).

Patients and therapists tend to organize current experiences in accordance with the primary thematic emotional patterns established in life

(Fosshage 2000). An essential point here is that both therapist and patient shape and influence the patient's transference experience. Bromberg (1998) suggests that "the transference/countertransference field may be thought of as an evolving blueprint of the patient's internal relational world as it is enacted with the therapist and is continually influenced by the two-way interaction" (p. 310). The patient's narrative recount of the salient and disturbing relational scenarios is not nearly as valuable therapeutically as recreating the emotional and relational dilemmas in the treatment relationship where new growth is possible.

A man presents for treatment secondary to a wish for love in his life. He aches to be an object of desire and fantasizes about these feelings and longings. He struggles to understand how he affects others and at work often finds himself in interpersonal predicaments, as others perceive him as overbearing. One of the first therapeutic hurdles involved conversations regarding the length of the treatment hour. My patient knew that some therapists conduct sessions for 55 or more minutes while I consistently adhered to a 50-minute hour. Many therapeutic conversations focused on my style of boundaries, inflexibility regarding session length, the meaning of my patient's repetitive request, and his sense of anger and injury at my unyielding stance. Having thoroughly explored and discussed the time boundary issue, we agree to disagree about the usefulness of my time boundary practices. I knew he felt the sessions were not long enough for him, and I sense he wishes I would make a special exception for him.

After an appointment in which I thought I ended the session on time, I leave my office and notice I had run over by 20 minutes. It was difficult to explain. Apparently, the batteries in my office clock were low, slowing down timekeeping. Startled by this awareness, my attention quickly turned to my patient as I wondered what meaning he would make of this event. By the end of the day, I received several distressed phone messages from my patient apologizing for making me run overtime. He worried what emotional or interpersonal backlash would follow. He felt certain his overbearing ways had bullied me into overtime the same way he sometimes emotionally ran over coworkers and then was socially and psychologically marginalized.

While longer sessions were just what my patient wanted, the treatment boundary and contract were established. This alteration in the length of the session created ambiguity and altered his sense of safety. He worried he had corrupted the therapeutic relationship with his longing, anger, and this event.

Treatment boundaries intend to protect the patient and the treatment process by ensuring that all interventions honor the fiduciary principle and place the patient's needs first. "When these boundaries are altered, what is allowed in the relationship becomes ambiguous. Such ambiguity is often experienced as an intrusion into the sphere of safety" (Peterson 1992, p. 74).

In this case, the alteration in boundaries without a therapeutic conversation and relational context stimulated this piece of his transference and a projective process. He worried he had done this to me and that I was enraged with him. This therapeutically rich event allowed my patient's inner relational world to be experienced and illuminated in our relationship. Subsequent dialogue allowed us to identify and gradually differentiate fantasy and perception. This event provided a valuable vehicle for deepening the therapeutic conversation about our relationship. We explored his fears of rupturing the relationship through his capacity to become self-absorbed and insistent upon his wishes at any interpersonal price.

An understanding of transference as co-constructed encourages therapists to pay closer attention to the meaning and contributing influence of verbal and nonverbal communications (Fosshage 2000). Essential therapeutic tasks include monitoring boundaries, the course of the treatment relationship, and attending to any potentially disruptive influences from within or between participants. Every action and nonaction by the therapist influences the relational field and the patient's construction of transference. Silence is an intervention.

A man attends a lecture I present and calls for a consultation. I am happy to meet with him and inquire what about the lecture or my person made him think I might be a good match. What did he notice? He disclosed that he thought I was "brilliant and capable of taking care of myself." I heard his admiring comment as a possible point of identification. Perhaps it also reflected a wish to be taken care of and not to have to take care of me. After the first consultation, he speaks to me in affectionate and familiar tones. Coining a pet name for me that rolls off his tongue as he says good-bye, it is as if we have a long history and a deep connection. In many ways, I know more about how he feels or wants to feel about me than I know about him. I sense he would like to feel close to me. He longs to have a deep connection with a woman whom he admires and respects and who has enough internal resources to both take care of herself and emotionally embrace him. Seeing and hearing me speak publicly about my work allowed this man to begin the transference relationship before he entered my office. He had some knowledge of me based on my lecture, and he readily assigned his emotional and relational scenarios from childhood. I quickly became the needed and missing relationship.

An empathic mirroring and genuinely curious stance that encourages him to chart the course of the sessions allows this initial transference to remain intact. Across a number of sessions, I learn that he was severely neglected by a mother who was self-absorbed and anxious, leaving little space for his self-development. His strongest childhood memories are of pleasing and placating mom, accompanied by his anger and a constant sense of disorganizing anxiety. His attachment to and idealization of me reflect a defensive shield against the depth of his emptiness, his unconscious longings to be cared for, and his terror around the intensity of feelings that will follow.

PROJECTIVE IDENTIFICATION

Bromberg (1998) comments that "with luck our patients' inner object world will emerge allowing what is really wrong to come forth" (p. 310). A relational approach to psychotherapy encourages our patients' patterns of relating to emerge in the treatment relationship, providing a window into their inner relational world. During my training, Paul Russell, a beloved teacher, commented that we depend on our patient's delivering her affective and relational dilemmas into the treatment relationship so that we might discover through our feelings where her development went awry (1983). Bromberg and Russell are highlighting the importance of transference as well as projective identification in the therapeutic process.

Projective identification refers to the experience of being overcome by "an intense feeling in response to a patient that is not being overtly presented by the patient" (Maroda 1999b, p. 481). Historically, projective identification was viewed as an unconscious defensive maneuver by the patient to rid herself of intolerable affects or self-representation by assigning the feelings to another person (Gabbard 1995, 1996; Maroda 1991, 1999a, 1999b; McLaughlin 1995; Ogden 1982, 1985, 1994). The use of this psychic mechanism was thought to represent an individual's deficits in affect tolerance and regulation.

Current understandings of projective identification view the process as a form of defense and as having an interpersonal and communicative focus. Stern's (1994) broader conceptualization of projective identification includes an attempt to establish a fantasized object relationship interpersonally through unconscious strategies. Also, it is thought to be a form of communication with the therapist about the patient's internal object world. The intent of the communication is to elicit responses that will be helpful in reintegrating projected feeling and self states.

A highly successful businessman comes for an initial psychotherapy appointment requesting assistance with a career decision. During a phone conversation before our meeting, he lets me know that as an adolescent he was psychiatrically hospitalized. That bad experience left him skeptical regarding psychotherapeutic work. A short time into the session, his state of consciousness shifts and he becomes mute, clearly dissociated, and falls into what appears to be a self-fragmented state. I am understandably alarmed and concerned for this man. Furthermore, I am not sure how to proceed, as I have little information about this patient and no clear ideas about what might be helpful. Then, my patient rises from his chair and walks out of the office into the waiting room and hovers in a corner. Now I am in a state of near terror and uncertainty myself. I follow this man to the waiting area trying to decide what to do.

Should I try to actively intervene and take control in some way? Maybe I should simply tell my patient to return to the office and sit down. I worry that my wish to control this patient is a shield against my own mounting feelings of anxiety and incompetence. I think better of it. Wrestling control from my patient seems like a bad idea because I worry that any active intervention will further frighten this patient. With no other data available to me, I move to a mirroring stance with my patient. I assume that my patient shares my sense of terror and worry that I might intervene in a hurtful manner. I begin to speak with my patient about my emotional experience. I comment, "I feel frightened and powerless. I see how distressed you are and I am afraid I don't have any idea about how to be helpful. Worse yet, I'm worried I'll say or do something that will make matters worse for you. Any clue you could give me about what you are experiencing would be helpful." With these comments, my patient began to share his experience at the moment and his worry about my judgment of him. The therapeutic conversation had begun.

The challenge for the therapist in these moments is to identify and contain the feelings for the patient. It requires resisting the sometimes overpowering temptation to translate these feelings into behavior or respond with like emotions. At moments, it is an impossible task. Frankly, as therapists we all have had the experience of blurting out some comment to a patient while overwhelmed with unwanted affect.

In difficult phases of psychotherapy, when affect becomes unbearable for the therapist or the patient, spontaneous self-disclosures may occur. Born out of frustration rather than formulation, these moments often provide therapeutic opportunities that otherwise would be lost. Sometimes these unsupervised, unconsciously stimulated comments help shift the affective tone in the therapeutic relationship and open up new dialogue. In other cases, therapists' expression of unmodulated, split-off affect injures and frightens patients, leaving them feeling unsafe and unprotected.

Several examples come to mind. Early in my career, a patient I had agreed to treat for a low fee turns out to be independently wealthy. As I attempt to negotiate a fee adjustment with my patient, who is calm and disinterested in this matter, I become angry at his devaluation of my services and person. Under the influence of his disavowed anger at being asked to pay his fair share and my annoyance at feeling devalued, I blurt out, "This is not volunteer work." At that time, I was intermittently plagued with self-doubts about my clinical skills, particularly during moments of intrapsychic or interpersonal stress. Often during those moments, I worried and wondered whether I was indeed worth my fee. My patient's unconscious anger and wish to be treated for free and my fragile sense of a competent professional self intersected, resulting in the strength of my annoyance. I regretted the unmodulated expression of my anger because it injured and frightened my patient. I wished I had framed the affective and relational dilemma between us with more self-control. The therapeutic work focused on this interaction for some time.

A colleague struggles to contain her anger and injury with a patient who relentlessly criticizes and responds to her with contempt. She has tried unsuccessfully to discuss this relational pattern with her patient, who refuses all efforts to examine his behavior or feelings. At a particularly difficult phase of the treatment when the therapist feels under siege, she blurts out, "I'm not sure how much longer I can work under these conditions." Her spontaneous disclosure of frustration matches her patient's aggression and captures her patient's attention. It also facilitates a new conversation concerning their relationship, his relational patterns, and his worries about connection.

Another colleague seeks consultation around a treatment in which the patient has been mute for prolonged periods of time in the treatment. The therapist in a moment of utter frustration comments, "This is stupid!" Feeling incompetent and powerless in the face of her patient's silence, the therapist understandably becomes angry as a shield against feelings of shame and the assault to her professional self-esteem. The patient hears this as "You are stupid!" Feeling unsafe in the therapeutic relationship, she elects to take time off from psychotherapy.

All therapists are vulnerable to these moments in therapeutic relationships. The therapeutic challenge and task is to stay connected to your inner experience, even when toxic, so that these feelings do not erupt into the therapeutic relationship in an unsupervised fashion. Easy to say, hard to do. The power of feelings and the challenge of not acting on these processes should not be understated. Our best hope is to be as compassionate and honest with ourselves as is humanly possible. Sustained empathic attention accompanied by self-inquiry sets the stage to revisit such exchanges with our patient with a fresh perspective.

Our patients need and want to know our affective state, and in particular how we feel with and about them. Patients inquire: "Will you let me know if you are angry with me?" "How will I be able to tell if I hurt your feelings?" "Will you tell me when you feel close to me?" A therapist's openness to fully experiencing and verbally validating her patients' emotional experience leads to developmentally useful conversations about emotional states.

Discussing disclosure of emotional states, Maroda (1991, 1999a, 1999b) emphasizes that therapists' modulated expression of affective states with patients is most helpful. Therapists' uncontrolled expression of affect most likely will frighten the patient and the therapist. Most therapists have had that experience. Therapists' unmodulated expression of affect with patients may indeed shame and frighten therapists. Such shame and anxiety may lead to a defensive retreat from a willingness to expose and discuss such transactions with patients. Our patients need us to hold and metabolize disowned affect and be willing to discuss and validate their perception and experience of themselves and us. While patients often accurately sense our emotional state, therapists must be willing to verbally validate patients' observations of the therapist's state (Maroda 1999a, 1999b). Consultation and peer support may be invaluable in sorting out the strands of mutual projective identification and the transference and countertransference.

ENACTMENT

Maroda (1999a, p. 124) defines enactment as "an affectively driven repetition of converging emotional scenarios from the patient's and therapist's lives." Enactment is a mutually cocreated interaction or event fueled by unconscious elements in both the patient and therapist. Davies and Frawley (1994) define the function of enactments as a means of unconsciously expressing dissociated aspects of self and object representations. From this perspective, the therapist's task is to remain fluid and follow the shifting dissociated communications. Remaining locked in to any single repetitive enactment that may become perseverative stifles movement in the relationship (Davies and Frawley 1994). In all of these models, enactments clearly serve therapeutic purposes.

A man has a severe reaction to my vacation, including life-threatening depression and homicidal rage. Upon my return, the therapeutic work is dominated by helping my patient contain and metabolize the flooding terror and sexualized rage stimulated by my absence. The intensity of my patient's sexual sadism is at times intolerable for me. I am relieved when his internal climate shifts to more tolerable feelings and the state of the transference follows. As we approach my next vacation, both my patient and I experience anticipatory anxiety. We recall how traumatizing and destabilizing my last absence was for him. He is again worried about managing without me but is filled with grief and sadness and appreciation for all my help.

As I notice the severity of this man's separation anxiety and how bereft he feels anticipating my absence, I am aware of my reluctance to offer him comfort. I feel unwilling to try to figure out with him how he might hold on to my presence and soothe himself in my absence. Supervising my feelings and behavior in sessions, I fantasize about how I might handle this case differently if the patient were female. I realize that my fear of my patient's sexual and aggressive feelings were unhelpful to him. This realization allows me to push past my feelings and explore with him his sadness and anxiety about my upcoming absence. My fearfulness that my patient will develop flooding sexual rage at me again led me to emotionally withdraw from him. My emotional withdrawal involved a countertransference wish to avoid an angry sexualizing man while my patient's contribution included a belief that caretakers will abandon and abuse him.

I initiated this mutually constructed scenario, which quickly became conscious secondary to my patient's shift in internal state. My nonaction, refusing to comfort him or get close to his distress, influenced his view of me and confirmed his feelings about himself and relationships. The subsequent negotiation around my vacation differentiated the therapy relationship from other life experiences for both my patient and myself.

Russell (1983) liked to comment that every successful psychotherapy involves a piece of psychotherapy for the therapist. He believed that a therapist's deep engagement with her patients always stimulates her own affects, vulnerabilities, and core conflicts. An open, clinically curious, compassionate stance with ourselves increases the likelihood of owning and reclaiming our own dissociated self-states and feelings.

Discussing mutual enactments, Hoffman (1992b) reminds us that it is often difficult to differentiate between new relational experiences and old repetitions. Old repetitions are contained in what appear to be new experiences, and new experiences are found in what seem to be simply old repetitions, as we can see in the previous case. Barely discernable shifts signal a moving along to new relational possibilities.

In the case of the dissociated businessman discussed earlier, presentation of a fragmented self-state represented an old repetition and new experience. As our conversation began in the waiting room, I recalled my patient told me that as an adolescent he had been labeled psychotic and committed to a psychiatric hospital. He correlates his dissociated episodes with being in psychotherapy and wonders if he should embark on another chapter of treatment or not.

Worrying and wondering about my judgment of him, he comments, "You must think I'm crazy." I comment, "I don't think you're crazy. I have a good idea of your many strengths, including a sense of how competent and accomplished you are in a professional domain. I know you have formed caring relationships with others. While I do not pretend to understand what you're up against here, I imagine if we were to work together that we would figure this out. I suspect that you have good reasons for your wordlessness and this altered state. Being in psychotherapy is a choice for you. You don't have to do this. It sounds as if these states are not so troublesome in your professional arena and you may choose to postpone this work. I am happy to assist you in any way that makes sense to you."

With these comments, my patient settled and shifted into a self-state that was more verbal and inclusive of other self-aspects. Therapists' clinical judgment is always relational and needs to be open to the full range of multiple realities that exist in any given moment between therapist and patient (Bromberg 1991, 1998). Allowing ourselves to occupy an intersubjective space with our patients opens up the possibility of experiencing and processing the full range of the patient's experience, including dissociated self-states.

In this case, the emergence of my patient's projective identification is accompanied by my efforts to identify and mindfully hold a more integrated and inclusive experience of the self. My efforts aim to both contain and fully experience my patient's dissociated self-experiences. This encounter was in part a negotiation around trust and my capacity to hold my patient's multiplicity of self-states without resorting to interventions aimed at coercive control. I refuse to join my patient in his experience of self as "crazy." It was reassuring to my patient that I believed he, in fact, had a choice about engaging in psychotherapy. I saw and held a wide range of his self-experience. The forced hospitalization scene was replayed in my waiting room. We were able to hold the multiplicity of his self-experience and negotiate meaning differentiating the past from this moment.

Enactment refers to the unconscious re-creation of past relational and affective patterns in the therapeutic relationship. "Enactments are crucial therapeutic events that constitute the very essence of treatment" (Aron 1996, p. 215). Psychotherapy that holds the promise of transforming an individual's sense of self, relational world, and affective experience relies upon enactment as a cornerstone of the therapeutic process and relationship. That is not to say that enactment is exclusively beneficial. Stolorow and Atwood (1992) discuss collusive intersubjective impasse, describing states of mutual enactment that threaten the analytic relational bond and process. In the preceding example involving my vacation, one can easily imagine how unhelpful to the patient the process might have been if my countertransference continued to dominate our interactions. Enactments hold the potential for great therapeutic gain as well as harm. For example, boundary violations commonly embody mutual projective identification and destructive enactments. Enactment in treatment relationships is ubiquitous and inevitable, and carries the seeds of transforming developmental and relational gains.

INTERNAL BOUNDARIES

Discussion of transference, projective identification, and enactment illustrates clearly that essential interpersonal and developmental data is communicated nonverbally between therapist and patient. Often, the therapist's internal experience offers the best clues to her patient's affective and relational experience. Mitchell (2000 p. 62) comments on "direct affect resonances" in therapeutic dyads, noting the "interpenetrability of transference-countertransference experiences." The value of viewing the therapist's affects as an opening into the disavowed or dissociated affective experiences of the patient is widely accepted (Benjamin 1998, 2002; Bollas 1987; Bromberg 1991, 1998; Mitchell 1991, 2000; Ogden 1982, 1994; Stern 1994, 2002). Within a clearly articulated treatment frame, a therapist examines and explores the full range of her inner experience with self and other. Analytic and relational writers discuss the need for permeable internal boundaries. Inner boundaries that allow the therapist to move with freedom from affect, to symbol, to associations are most helpful (Aron 1996; Benjamin 1998; Ehrenberg 1992; Gabbard 1995; Gabbard and Lester 1995; Maroda 1991, 1999a; Mitchell 2000; Ogden 1994).

Elaborating on contemporary relational theories, Mitchell (2000, p. 63) describes the self as "multiplicitous, not a single self . . . but discontinuous, multiple self-organizations packaged together by an illusory sense of continuity and coherence . . ." Permeable internal boundaries are necessary for grasping fully and understanding the rich array of the patient's self-other experiences and our interactive influence. With practice and support, a therapist learns to trust her intuition, rely upon *implicit relational knowing* (Stern et al. 1998), and allow herself to deeply engage with the multiplicity of her own and her patient's experience.

Psychotherapy relies on a therapist's careful attention to the unfolding of the therapeutic relationship, the development of the transference/countertransference, and upon her inner experience to inform her therapeutic work. The patient's experience with the therapist as with others is "enormously dense and complex, with many different facets" (Mitchell 2000, p. 66). The therapist's inner experience will reflect valuable data about herself as well as the patient's development, inner experience, and the state of the therapeutic relationship. Recognition and use of her own subjectivity in negotiating the therapeutic relationship is a mainstay of practice, allowing the therapist to gather in dissociated experiences.

Inner restrictions or conflicts regarding what feelings and fantasies are permissible for a therapist to experience regarding a patient are an obstacle to deep engagement and participation in relational repetitions and repair. Sexual attraction, love, anger, contempt, and disgust are feelings that therapists commonly are conflicted about experiencing toward patients. Such feelings may stimulate shame. Hoffman (2002) reminds us that a therapist must come to terms with her own investment in not being a "bad object." Our deep investment in doing good and being appreciated leaves us vulnerable to disavowal and dissociation of negative self-states and toxic affects. I encourage therapists to experiment with developing an intimate relationship with her inner feelings and fantasies around her clinical work. While for some therapists this position may be novel or present special challenges, this personal professional journey is mandatory if one is to conduct psychotherapy. Personal treatment as well as professional mentors may assist a therapist with developing these capacities.

Inner barriers or conflict around particular affects prevent the therapist from empathic joining and resonating with the patient's affective and unspoken experience. With restricted access to her inner affective and fantasy life regarding her patients, a therapist loses valuable clinical data about her patient, the therapeutic work, and herself. Furthermore, she runs the risk of unacknowledged or destabilizing affects and disavowed identifications influencing detrimentally her clinical work and the therapeutic relationship. Denied, distorted, or dissociated affects and self-experiences by therapists increase the risk of behavioral enactments that may be harmful.

Therapists resist surrendering to patients and their own dissociated self-aspects and commingling of identifications to avoid destabilizing affects and the associated anxiety. Fully engaging with our patients involves receptivity to activation of our early, perhaps noxious identifications. The commingling of identifications taxes the therapist and challenges the relational process. These moments are characterized by rapid reversal of identifications and great relational turbulence.

Common dangers include countertransference dominance, control struggles, and relational disconnection that may become manifest in subtle and not so subtle emotional withdrawal away from the patient and into the self. What we hope may be a deep, potentially transforming, relational engagement with our patient may become a destructive entanglement resulting in therapeutic stalemate and impasse. Therapists resist the tug of such deep engagements with patients for good reasons; it is much easier to get into such engagements and far more challenging to construct a useful path through to an altered relational experience for both patient and therapist.

Davies (2002), in a recent lecture discussing repetition and repair in therapeutic relationships, notes that the therapist must be willing to fully occupy the countertransference. By that, Davies means the therapist must be willing to both hold the patient's dissociated self-aspects and surrender to her own dissociated self-aspects. Toxic affects and self-states may be intolerable for therapists, stimulating shame and guilt. To ward off shame and guilt, a therapist disconnects from her inner experience and evacuates these toxic affects as "not me," assigning them to her patient.

These moments are accompanied by a collapse of self-reflective functioning that forecloses the full affective array of self-other experiences. As therapists, we strive to open up space for multiple self-other experiences, moving fluidly from one self-other configuration to another in the therapeutic relationship (Benjamin 2002; Bromberg 1998; Davies 2002; Hoffman 2002; Ogden 1994). Surrendering to our experience provides the psychic relational space that allows for the multiplicity of our self-other experiences. With surrender, the temptation to polarize these relational moments into you versus me, a "do to or be done to" frame may be resisted (Benjamin 2002). Traumatic reenactments involve mutuality and deep relational engagement of disavowed affects and identifications for both therapist and patient (Benjamin 1998; Davies 2002; Gabbard 1995; B. Pizer 1998; S. A. Pizer 2000; Stern 2002; Stolorow and Atwood 1992).

With this frame, moments of impasse in therapeutic relationships are conceptualized as "nascent enactments," enactments not fully developed or elaborated (Davies 2002). In such cases, the therapist defends against the shameful and toxic feelings. Unwilling to go there spiritually with her patient, she removes herself from the mutual relational experience. Relational repair and healing occur when the therapist is willing to deeply engage in the repetition and the mutual enactment with the patient. Gradually, therapist and patient fully elaborate the multiplicity of meaning and work through the enactment.

Benjamin (1998) pushes us beyond the "seesaw of complementarity, in which we incessantly reverse positions through identifications with patients." She constructs a mental space, *the third*, that allows us to move in and out of such entanglements (p. xiv). Elaborating an intersubjective perspective, she reaches beyond the dyad and creates a third position—a space that is able to avoid polarized self-relational experiences. The third involves mutual recognition that "it takes one to know one." Furthermore, it gives birth to an internal mental space through dialogue that recognizes the subjectivity of the self, the other, and difference. It leaves a space for the therapist to surrender to her experience, including impotence, despair, and rage, and occupy the position of observer. Thirdness opens up space for multiple truths and dialogue that occurs outside the web of identifications (Benjamin 1998). Benjamin's construct of thirdness provides a conceptual pathway that guides therapists as they fully engage with their patients in repetition and repair moving along to new procedural knowledge and an altered sense of self and other.

I will share a psychotherapy case from the early years of my practice that illustrates well both the untoward effects and the ultimate benefits of gathering in and employing denied and dissociated affects by a therapist.

A thirty-five-year-old man, depressed and panic stricken, comes for treatment after his six-year-old son is psychiatrically hospitalized with suicidal ideation. The development of the therapeutic relationship is painstaking because this man is terrified of self and others. He lives with a deadening inner emptiness. He has managed unmanageable self-states and flooding affect through compartmentalization and dissociation. Slowly this man develops a deep attachment to me and comes to feel seen and emotionally held in my presence. As a very lengthy vacation absence approaches, my patient becomes more depressed and suicidal. I do my best to assist my patient with his sense of terror, grief, and anger at my impending absence before I depart with mixed results. We concoct a range of transitional devices in an attempt to keep our emotional and relational connection alive while we are apart.

Upon my return, my patient arrives for our appointment dressed in black, death-like, and silent. After a brief hello, he sits silently during our sessions, disconnected from me and I assume from himself. We sit alone together several times a week for many weeks. I focus on him and my internal experience trying to decipher his feeling state. I am awash in a sense of emptiness and sadness. The recurring themes involve a sense of helplessness and anxiety.

I begin speaking more, offering theories about him and his internal state. My theories focus on the meaning of our relationship and the disruption in our connection precipitated by my absence. He both wants to be present and not, worries about destroying our relationship and wants to punish me. I comment, "Your anger and hurt about my absence is unspeakable, but we both feel it. Perhaps you are protecting me from the full expression of your anger about my absence. You are worried about destroying our connection with your anger and longing." Or, "You are punishing yourself and me for letting me be so important to you. It made my absence unbearable." Or, "When you feel this hurt and angry, you disconnect from yourself and me." Or, "Maybe this is a test of my care and commitment to you. You will be here in the flesh only. You refuse to give me your emotional self again." Or, "You felt powerless around my absence, and now I am powerless to help you with these overwhelming feelings. It feels awful." Nothing seems to resonate with my patient or be of help.

In a session where apparently I felt too connected to him or am working too hard to win him, he turns his chair around and sits with his back facing me. It is an angry, childlike behavior, but he doesn't leave the room. I experience it as a powerful communication regarding his opposing internal forces. Primarily, I believe he wants me to experience the loss of control and disconnection involved in my absence for him. He wants me to hold the overpowering feelings of powerlessness and rage. I get it!

Weeks later, I need to change an appointment, as I plan to be out of town part of the week. The day of his rescheduled appointment, I neglect to take my appointment book to my hospital office and forget we have an appointment. During his rescheduled appointment, I sit in my office catching up on paperwork as he sits in the waiting room. I check my messages before I leave for the day and receive a written note from my patient, "I was here and waited for an hour, where were you?" I reach my patient by phone later that day and comment, "I am very sorry I forgot your appointment today. I was in my office, but I left my appointment book elsewhere. I understand you waited for me. This error could not have come at a worse time. I'm sorry and I hope we can discuss it next week."

Before the next appointment, my patient sends me a letter saying "I believe your behavior speaks louder than your words. I'm worried you are fed up with me. I'm so ungrateful, so unpleasant to be around. You don't have to work with me anymore if you don't want to. What's going on with you? I want to know." Ashamed, guilty, embarrassed by my lapse, I realize I had reached an internal threshold around feeling inept and frustrated with this man and our work together. I had not allowed myself to acknowledge the depth of my sense of powerless and frustration. My split-off, unconscious feelings of frustration fueled this behavioral enactment.

Clearly, my countertransference was stimulated in large part by his provocative behavior and the intensity of his unspoken experience that intersected with my unrealistic and ultimately unhelpful ideals as a young therapist. A cognitive conceptual understanding of countertransference anger made intuitive sense to me. However, I was reluctant to experience these feelings with a patient with whom I also felt a deep connection. This may in part be explained by my clinical youth, but I was also aware that I simply could not bear to let myself go there emotionally. I did not want to be angry or resentful toward my patients.

After receiving my patient's letter, I could see that my patient needed a response from me about my feelings and behavior. Clearly, it would not be helpful to solely focus on my patient's experience. Also, I felt a sense of obligation to take responsibility for my behavior and to try to understand how it might be useful in our work together. In the next appointment, I comment, "I am sorry I hurt and frightened you by forgetting our appointment. I know I added to your anguish. It was not your fault or your responsibility. It was my error. I have thought about it, and I agree it was about more than forgetting my appointment book. My lengthy vacation and your feelings around my absence have been painful and disruptive to you and to our work. It has been hard for us to reconnect. When angry, you distance and disconnect from yourself and from me. It's been hard for me to know how to be helpful. It would have been better if this came to me in another way, but I feel my behavior was a signal to me that I was carrying more than my share of our work. I wish I had noticed this feeling and spoken with you about it. You and I were both communicating nonverbally. I want you to know I am committed to working with you."

After this event and my apology, my patient reconnected and began to speak with me about his experience. We focused on the trauma of my absence, his experience in sessions while not speaking, and the meaning to him of my forgetting his appointment. Ultimately, my capacity to withstand his rage and ignore my own experience of feeling burdened was unhelpful. Looking back over this experience many years later, I realize that my inability to acknowledge and feel my patient's and my own anger led to the behavioral enactment. But I also believe it prolonged the silent sessions and a kind of therapeutic stalemate. It would have been more useful to address his feelings and my experience from an intrapsychic as well as a relational perspective early on. If I had been able to fully embrace my internal experience and accept this cocreated scene, an emotionally honest and dyadic stance might have been more possible. The shame and guilt surrounding my experience of anger toward my patient complicated and confused the matter.

BOUNDARY CROSSINGS

A boundary crossing may be understood as any action that disrupts the treatment frame and the therapeutic relationship. Boundary crossings represent enactments between therapist and patient that may or may not be harmful to the therapeutic process.

> A man in later life comes for psychotherapy requesting help with identification and management of feeling states, boundaries, and intimacy issues. A lengthy previous treatment with a female psychiatrist, while somewhat useful, was ultimately not helpful with these developmental concerns. During the course of that psychotherapy there were many instances of role reversal between my patient and his psychiatrist. Numerous boundary crossings and violations received little therapeutic attention. While the patient was at times frustrated at the lack of progress on substantive issues, the mutually idealizing relationship felt familiar. It provided an illusion of comfort, as it often mirrored his childhood relationship with each parent in differing ways. After a series of crises in his marriage that were fueled by these unresolved developmental issues, he sought treatment with me.
>
> Engaging readily and deeply with me, my patient is hungry to receive much-needed and deserved therapeutic assistance with troubling and confusing feeling states and accompanying behaviors. Deeply relieved that

"I am in charge, in a good way," he settles into our relationship and the therapeutic work. He begins to trust that I will be the therapeutic rudder, commenting, "You are hard, but in a good way. You have empathy for my feelings but not my self-deception. You see things I can't yet see. I feel like I lost so many years in that other therapy, and now I want to move along."

A mainstay of the therapeutic work focuses upon our relationship and issues of safety and trust. Can he trust the feelings of care and comfort he experiences with me? Is his anger and disappointment dangerous or destructive to relationships as well as to himself? Can he allow himself to bear longings and wishes without stimulating self-contempt or undue anxiety? Can he ask for what he wants and needs?

Writing this book adds to my professional schedule and impedes my timely attention to clinical paperwork. My billing is late, and on one occasion there is an error in my patient's favor. While he is distressed by my billing error, he tries to soldier on. He does not make much of a fuss because the feelings stimulate such shame and guilt and because he feels so cared for and helped by me. Structuring a process wherein he allows himself to share the full range of his experience around the billing, we explore the meaning of my lapses to him and our relationship. Anxiety and anger are stimulated as my patient experiences these lapses as boundary crossings. He worries that I will become inattentive or abandon my other therapeutic functions as well. Fractures in my take-charge, competent style evoke disruptive memories. It stirs the fantasy that perhaps he will lose me as he has known me, and I will begin to feel and behave like his previous therapist.

My billing error came in close proximity to his planned vacation and then my planned vacation, which only added to his feelings of distress. Perhaps I was not who I appeared to be and could not be trusted to care deeply for him? The fact that I committed an indisputable error, by not billing him for several hours of therapy, facilitated the direct expression of his painful feelings and worries. Through continued dialogue, we explored alternate ways of making meaning of this event including the possibility that competent, admired others lapsed on occasion. Maybe he did not have to have so many rules enforced by such a harsh self-critic.

Across the conversation, I comment, "I'm sorry my late and erroneous billing has so frightened and angered you. It is not your job to stay on top of my billing. I will be more attentive. It's a good sign that you know what you're feeling and can be so direct with me. I know how much you dislike being angry and angry with me. I wonder if my error left you feeling not cared for and unimportant to me." He responds, "You forgot to bill for hours that were important and meaningful to me. I remember what we discussed and how helpful it was to me. It does make me feel like you don't care. What if I noticed and didn't tell you?"

My billing errors set the stage for my patient to reenact scenes from his previous unhelpful treatment and his childhood experience, allowing new material and feelings to be explored and negotiated. Through sustained engagement with the layers of complex meaning evoked by this lapse, my patient and I gradually coconstruct meaning and reestablish a sense of safety in the therapeutic relationship. My taking full responsibility for my contribution to this scenario helped shift an unhelpful reenactment into a useful therapeutic conversation.

Gabbard and Lester (1995) offer a number of guidelines to assist a therapist in distinguishing boundary crossings from the more harmful boundary violations. Therapists usefully pose the following questions to analyze these transactions in therapeutic relationships.

> Does the therapist catch oneself as the enactment is unfolding? Does the therapist regain conscious self-supervisory control? Is the enactment an isolated occurrence? Is it repetitive and unresponsive to the therapist's own efforts? Does the therapist have the capacity to discuss and analyze the incident with her patient? Discussion of the event may determine whether it is ultimately productive or harmful to the patient or the therapeutic process. (Gabbard and Lester 1995, p. 127)

Therapists need to recognize boundary crossings and violations with patients and take responsibility for repairing the relationship (R. Epstein 1994; Gabbard and Lester 1995). If the therapist has crossed a line and the therapeutic dyad is unable to discuss the event, it will be difficult to repair or determine the extent of harm. Epstein (1994) outlines the multistep process for attending to boundary violations and repairing injuries.

> First, the therapist attends to the patient's experience including thoughts, feelings, and fantasies to elicit conscious and unconscious reactions to the therapist's behavior. Next, the therapist acknowledges her contribution to

the incident and finally, the therapist helps the patient metabolize the psychological and emotional aftermath of any injury. (R. Epstein 1994, p. 116)

In the preceding clinical vignettes, I structured a process focused on repairing an injury and optimizing the possibility of turning a therapeutic error into a therapeutic opportunity.

BOUNDARY VIOLATIONS

Therapists possess great power and authority in the treatment relationship, power that may be used for the patient's good or for irreparable harm. Boundary violations are an egregious and potentially harmful transgression of the therapeutic contract and treatment frame that involve a breach of the fiduciary contract and abuse of the therapist's power (L. Epstein 1995; Gabbard and Lester 1995; Peterson 1992; Strasburger et al. 1991). Professional sexual misconduct is a very damaging and all too common example of an egregious boundary violation (Gabbard 1989; Herman et al. 1987).

There are many less-dramatic instances of practices that constitute harmful transgressions. While professional ethics boards decide ultimately what is ethical conduct, the intrapsychic meaning to the patient determines whether an interaction has been a boundary violation or not (Gabbard and Lester 1995; Waldinger 1994). While engaged in individual psychotherapy, a young woman recovered memories of childhood sexual abuse by a male family member. A serious depression and acute symptoms of Post Traumatic Stress Disorder develop, and the patient seeks a psychopharmacology consultation. During the psychopharmacology consultation, the psychiatrist lounged on the couch in his office. During the examination he asked the woman how she feels about her breasts. This was not a question she imagined encountering from an unknown physician during a psychopharmacological evaluation. Failing to take a medical history, the psychiatrist, nevertheless, gave her a prescription for an antidepressant. The patient experienced the question about her breasts as an inappropriate and egregious boundary violation. She felt the experience exasperated her symptoms of PTSD and filed a complaint with an ethics committee. After investigation, the committee determined the physician's conduct included an incident of substandard care. He failed to obtain a medical history before prescribing medications. The "inappropriate" question about the patient's breasts was assessed as an example of insensitive, idiosyncratic care but not misconduct. In the patient's mind, the experience was unequivocally a harmful boundary violation. The ethics committee recommended one year of mandatory clinical supervision for the psychiatrist.

Earlier in my career, I hoped and believed that the incidence of professional sexual misconduct might diminish through primary prevention efforts. I hoped that by educating therapists regarding the technical handling of intense affects in the treatment relationship the incidence of professional sexual misconduct would decrease. While I remain committed to advocating for the inclusion of such curriculum in professional training, my hopes that education will diminish misconduct evaporate as I understand more about how vulnerable we are as therapists and how great the human capacity is to delude oneself. Recently, after his patient filed a complaint, a highly respected and well-known analyst admitted to violating sexual boundaries with his patient. While I have no way of knowing, I imagine this man, who was known to be in a vulnerable state secondary to serious health issues, isolated himself and his practice with this patient, precisely because the feelings were so pleasurable and distracting.

Under the right circumstances we are all vulnerable to potentially dangerous self-deception. Even with a commitment to honor the fiduciary principle, therapists consciously and unconsciously use power in the treatment relationship, on occasion in a self-serving manner. A practice of regularly presenting one's work and seeking consultation is a protective and instructive practice for all therapists. A clearly articulated frame protects the patient and the therapeutic process, as well as the therapist, during moments of intensity and confusion. The incidence of professional sexual misconduct and nonsexual boundary violations well documents just how challenging it may be for a therapist to contain her feelings and maintain therapeutic boundaries.

As therapists, we need to stay connected to our affective experience and take responsibility for our feelings and behavior with our patients.

During a heated interpersonal moment in a session, as a patient tries to both seduce me and articulate her own feelings, I startle with anxiety and internally shut down. I nonverbally signal to my patient that this conversation and her feelings were off limits. I cannot help myself and follow up with a didactic comment about the therapeutic contract that injures my patient and stifles the exploration of her feelings. In a subsequent session, my courageous patient shares her anger and her experience that I had used my power in a hurtful manner to control her and her expression of feeling. She comments, "I don't feel safe with you. That was a power trip." I knew my patient was correct, and I was genuinely sorry that I had injured and frightened her: "I'm sorry. I can see how unhelpful that conversation was. I will study this and try to get a better understanding of what happened in that session. Let's talk about how it felt to you and what it meant." I realize that I, as well as my patient, was frightened by the intensity of feelings and was internally trying to control my identification by distancing myself with a harsh, inner stance. Although I unconsciously chose the stance in this moment, it was influenced by my patient's stimulation. Choreographed unconsciously, this injury provided a window into the ways in which my patient had previously felt overpowered or violated in relationships. It also offered an opportunity to begin to differentiate the therapeutic relationship as a potentially different and healing connection.

Such moments are to be expected. A compassionate, yet self-scrutinizing attitude by the therapist allows these moments to be discussed and negotiated with her patient. As they sort out the meaning and effect upon her patient, the therapist accepts responsibility for her contribution. Nonsexual boundary crossings and enactments are ubiquitous in therapeutic work. Often these events provide invaluable vehicles for deepening the therapeutic conversation, allowing for new understandings of self and other.

Therapists who deny or minimize the power differential between therapist and patient will be unable to monitor their own use and misuse of power in the therapeutic relationship. Alternatively, therapists who subscribe to an authoritarian, all-knowing therapeutic style may be insensitive to power issues in the therapeutic relationship. It is precisely because of the intimate and intense nature of the therapeutic relationship that a therapist must monitor her feelings, supervise her clinical choices, and seek consultation. Psychotherapy may be an emotionally arousing, potentially destabilizing relationship for both participants. Damaging boundary violations committed by otherwise competent clinicians are often the result of a therapist's inability to notice her participation in an enactment. Or it may represent a therapist's inability to identify and contain arousing and destabilizing affects and disavowed identifications. As therapists, we are all vulnerable to these conditions and capable of distorting, denying, or rationalizing conduct with particular patients when in these altered states.

❷

BOUNDED INTIMACY

Psychotherapy for most patients is a destination of last resort. After they have tried everything they can think of to help themselves, they turn to us. The first therapeutic task is to create enough safety so that the person may begin to share her story and her feelings in the service of developing a therapeutic relationship. Often, my patient hopes I will share some insight, offer a course of action, or teach her about human nature—all of which I, of course, hope to do from time to time. However, the affective and relational aspects of the therapeutic relationship will be of far greater significance to my patient than any cognitive piece of information I share. It may take some time before my patient understands this.

GUIDING CONCEPTS AND THEORY OF THERAPEUTIC ACTION

I endorse a hybrid model of therapeutic action that honors both traditional concepts and processes such as transference/countertransference, projective identification, and enactment. Infant research and developmental theories of attachment and affect regulation inform this perspective as well. An eclectic approach to therapeutic work allows me to borrow from both traditional psychoanalytic theory and more recent developmental theory that emphasizes an intersubjective perspective.

Essential concepts from traditional theory that organize and inform my work with patients include the belief that the relationship is the vehicle of therapeutic action, and that the reliving and metabolizing of feelings in the therapeutic relationship is the process that holds the potential for transforming change (Davies 1994a, 1994b, 2000; Ehrenberg 1992; Gabbard 1995, 1996; Maroda 1991, 1999a, 1999b; Mitchell 1988, 1997, 2000; Orbach 2000).

Creating a safe place for the unfolding of the therapeutic relationship involves a therapist's willingness to remain fluid and open to influence (Havens 1989, 1996). A willingness to "throw away the book," to do "something fresh and creative," and engage in radical maneuvers is essential if we are to bring a new perspective to our patient's experience of self and other, and not simply offer a repetition of old relational scenarios (Fonagy and Target 1998; Hoffman 1994).

Humor, spontaneity, and allowing oneself the freedom to play in the intersubjective space creates the possibility of authentic improvisational moments that offer special instances of being known and seen. Such moments involve imaginative engagement with patients that conveys deep recognition of the other (Ringstrom 2001).

Important developmental concepts derived from infant-mother studies include the *fitting together* processes that constitutes relational attunement, the specificity of being known, and the fundamental role of the therapeutic relationship to impart new and expanded *relational procedural knowledge* (Lyons-Ruth et al. 1998; Lyons-Ruth 1999, 2000, 2004; Sander 2002; Stern et al. 1998; Tronick et al. 1998).

Procedural knowledge refers to "knowing how to do something, how to behave, rather than knowing information" (Lyons-Ruth 2004).* Relational procedural knowledge signifies the patient's nonverbal internal representation of implicit procedures for how one conducts a relationship. The development of new meaning and relational systems for patients is acquired through unconscious pathways and verbal interactions

---

*This text is not yet in print.

leading to more complex and coherent relational procedural forms of knowing. Therapeutic change is the result of slow, repetitive relational transactions that expand affective consciousness and rearrange a patient's internal implicit understandings of how to be with another.

As therapist, I focus my attention on expressed and unacknowledged affects to deeply understand my patient's feeling state and subjective experience. The therapeutic relationship and the negotiation of feelings are the medium of healing and change. The establishment of a safe intersubjective space between therapist and patient allows the patient to experience emotions and self-states in the presence of a caring, curious, and concerned other (Fonagy 1999, 2001; Fonagy et al. 2002). A bounded, intimate relationship with a therapist that succeeds in establishing mutual trust and willingness by both participants to be open and vulnerable holds the promise of developmental possibilities (Aron 1996; Davies 2000, 2002; Ehrenberg 1992; McLaughlin 1995). Fixed internal patterns of relating become visible in the therapeutic relationship, while work in the transference highlights the differences between self and other. The giving up of defensive shields and an emotional opening up to oneself in a trusting relationship is self-altering (Maroda 1991, 1999a, 1999b; Russell 1976a, 1976b, 1976c, 1976d, 1976e, 1983). This may only occur if the therapist is willing to be vulnerable and emotionally honest as well.

An understanding of the need for patients to relive developmental dramas in the therapeutic relationship, including disruption and repair of self-object injuries, is essential. Externalization of intolerable affects and disowned self-states by both patient and therapist are challenging and ubiquitous. The holding and containing functions of the therapeutic frame and relationship are central. Boundary dilemmas, enactments, and the negotiation of intense emotions are anticipated and viewed as therapeutically valuable (Gabbard and Lester 1995; Russell 1983; Stolorow and Atwood 1992; Stolorow et al. 1997; Teicholz and Kreigman 1998).

A therapist's self-revelatory stance that rests upon authentic engagement is accompanied by a willingness to be known and seen in the process. For the therapist, this includes sharing information about thoughts, feelings, and one's internal processes. Studying the patient's experience of emotions and self-states is coupled with focusing the patient on the therapist's mental states and processes to highlight differences and ultimately shift internal representations (Fonagy 1999).

Gradually, through deep relational engagement, the re-creation of the patient's internal object world in the transference/countertransference occurs. A renegotiation of the repetition within the therapeutic relationship offers hope of reparation, emotional growth, and new procedural knowledge. The transforming power of such a relational experience with a therapist allows the individual to experience and develop new aspects of the self and to expand and deepen affective competence. The full engagement of a patient's transference is inevitable and necessary for change. However, I also focus on working against the transference, discovering the relational scenarios that foreclose my patient's developing a more inclusive, integrated feeling and knowing of self and other.

A developmental relational framework endorses the therapeutic value of enactment and working through in the therapeutic relationship as well as nonlinguistic processes involved in relational skill acquisition. Nonlinguistic processes may be more developmentally valuable and reparative than interpretative interventions. Both renegotiation of the repetition and shifts in ways of being are central to therapeutic change.

With this approach, the therapist is emotionally available and able to offer the patient the opportunity for developing a new, healing relationship. Damaging developmental and relational dramas are reenacted in a safe interpersonal space. Along with the opportunity for healing, the therapeutic relationship provides an arena for acquiring experience and detailed information about how to conduct a close, collaborative relationship (Lyons-Ruth 2000, 2004; Sander 2002; Stern et al. 1998).

An integrated model presents the therapist with certain theoretical challenges concerning the specificity of therapeutic action. What produces change? Is change the result of reliving and metabolizing affect and negotiating historic relational scenarios in the context of a new healing relationship? From this perspective, change occurs intrapsychically and moves to the external and interpersonal. The patient comes to feel and experience the self and other in new ways and as a result interacts differently in the world. Or does the change result from novel interpersonal transactions through which the patient acquires new relational moves that alter her internal states and experience of the self and other?

Although there is no consensus, I propose elements of both models are necessary for change. From observations in my practice, I believe that patients must feel better, stronger, and different enough about themselves and others to be able to take risks. As a result they engage in new and different ways with themselves and in the world of others. Patients who hold themselves in new ways take relational risks, signifying an internal shift away from noxious identifications. This shift is an indication that the patient has engaged in the process of identification with the therapist. Engaging in new relational transactions results in an altered sense of self and a more inclusive and coherent affective experience. From this view, shifts in ways of being and feeling follow experience, not precede the new experience. Patients try out new moves with us and then take these relational moves and altered sense of self into the world.

THE SPECIFICITY OF BEING KNOWN AND EXPANDING AND REARRANGING RELATIONAL PROCEDURAL KNOWLEDGE

Based on infant-mother studies of attachment, Sander (2002) proposes that therapist and patient negotiate a series of "essential adaptational tasks of fitting together." These tasks lay the foundation for both being known and developing new ways of being with another. Fitting together is a complex process of trial and error that involves the therapist's willingness to rapidly shift through a series of self-other configurations in search of the language, the tone, or the particular stance that works or seems to fit with this particular patient (Lyons-Ruth 1999, 2000, 2004; Sander 2002). These relational moves are chosen largely unconsciously and shaped by the therapist's intuition and sense of the patient in any given moment. Through this painstaking trial-and-error process, therapists discover and select the language and relational postures that are uniquely tailored to the specifics of this therapeutic dyad.

Parenting scenarios with infants capture the improvisational nature and the complexity involved in identifying relational maneuvers that facilitate fitting together with a particular patient. The physical and affective maneuvering that parents shift through trying to soothe and comfort irritable infants illustrates well this fitting-together process. Consider this scenario: Many infants experience affective disequilibrium during late afternoon or early evening hours and sometimes cry for extended periods of time. Often, soothing efforts begin with attempts to feed the infant. If there is no reduction in crying, the caretaker rapidly proceeds through a series of other maneuvers aimed at settling down a cranky infant. These maneuvers may include rocking the infant cradled in your arms or placing the infant on your right shoulder and patting her back. If there is no reduction in irritability, the parent may switch the infant to another position. Many efforts are not effective and are discarded. With trial and error, the caretaker discovers that singing to the infant while propping her on your left shoulder in fact soothes this infant, and she settles. Each subsequent evening, the infant's crankiness will now be greeted with soothing efforts that begin with singing to the infant while she is propped on your left shoulder. These maneuvers will be selected out as having "worked."

Lyons-Ruth (2004) comments that "this slow and idiosyncratic process of improvising and selecting particular relational fittings-together that will be elaborated at the expense of others lays the foundation for the emergence of new ways of being together." This process occurs with our patients as well. Fitting-together tasks include "specificity of recognition of the patient's inner awareness, purpose, and intention shaping conscious organization" (Sander 2002, p. 30). The therapeutic dyad "builds increasingly inclusive and coherent moments of recognition between themselves" (Lyons-Ruth 2004).

With attention to this intersubjective space, therapist and patient may cocreate a depth of knowing and being known that is novel and that rearranges self-organization. Sometimes sitting with a patient, I sense that I know her mind and what she is about to say in advance, and, in fact, I do know. Or a patient and I simultaneously smile, sensing that we are thinking the same thought or are about to make the same comment. Sometimes I borrow my patient's language, and sometimes she borrows my language. Sometimes we are thinking of language that is familiar and unique to our relationship that we have developed together. Or a patient relates to me his fantasy of my internal dialogue about a particular matter, and I am struck with the accuracy and specificity of his knowing. In fact, his narrative captures my internal process well, and in response, I say to him, "You know me so well."

This process of being seen and of expanding affective consciousness reorders conscious organization, bringing the patient's "true self" and "agency-to-initiate" to new levels of validity and competence (Sander 2002, p. 11).

A woman arrives for an individual session after an emotionally intense and stirring group psychotherapy session. In the group, she shared, uncharacteristically, the depth of her sadness and allowed herself to receive comfort. Tentatively, maybe anxiously, she enters my office and questions playfully, "I guess you don't want to do the talking today?" I comment playfully back, "I guess *you* don't want to do the talking today. That's the story." She sits silently. I comment, "Maybe you're worried what will come out here, like in the group." With energy I continue, "Turn your internal supervisor off and who knows what will emerge!" She laughs with recognition and excitement and comments, "Oh my God! Like in the group. What a shock! I can't believe it. It's not me." I respond, "Maybe it's a new you. The developing you. So brave of you to allow yourself to be so vulnerable." She responds, "Usually I'm in such control." I say, "I know. You're so adept at that. That's what makes me think you were relinquishing control, maybe unconsciously, allowing other longings and feelings to surface. You were trying something new. What was risky about this for you?" She responds, "I don't like the attention. I could have cried for forty minutes. People were so supportive. It makes me think about my mother. I never wanted her to be nice to me." I inquire, "How come?" She responds, "Well, then when she was mean again it hurt so much more." I respond, "The predictable hurt and disappointment with your mother led you to disconnect from your feelings and longings for care as a way to avoid that pain. As a child, the depth of your disappointment and longing was unbearable. You had to turn away from yourself and relationships. You are stronger now, know so much more about yourself and your feelings, and are better able to manage disappointment."

She responds, "Because of this group, I'm able to be much freer in other groups, like at my volunteer job. I'm there, present emotionally, and feel so good. It's a new me. Never been like this before. I like the people. They like me. I'm in my own skin, emotionally present. A woman said to me, 'Wow, you really listen.'" I respond, "That comment meant so much to you." She continues, "Yes, such a compliment. Nobody would have said that before. I was so internally occupied. I couldn't listen, disconnected from others and myself."

With this group and me internally in residence, this woman takes relational risks holding herself in new ways in the group and in the outside world. Learning new relational moves both through verbal exchanges and unconscious identification, her fund of knowledge about how to advance in relationships expands. As in this case, doing something different, trying out new relational behavior, leads to broader and more integrated affective experience and an altered sense of self.

The therapeutic relationship provides patients with essential information regarding knowing "what to do" and "how to do."

A patient comes in with editorial comments about a written piece focused on our work together. At the time, I do not feel well and clearly am not at my best. He begins with "You're probably not going to like this," maybe sensing my diminished capacities and the strength of his negative feelings. He proceeds to detail changes he would like me to make concerning the last sentence of the piece to which he has a strong feeling of dislike. With energy, he repetitively states his case for why that sentence is substandard and, in his view, must be changed.

While I acknowledge that he has a legitimate point of view, I am struck by the affect driving his commentary and am puzzled. I comment,

"I'm puzzled. I can't quite figure out what about this sentence has stimulated your response and feelings. How are you making meaning of this?" I inquire, "Is it hard for you that your therapist does not write as well as you do? Will you feel embarrassed or ashamed knowing there are some crummy sentences in this piece, that somehow my writing skills reflect poorly upon you?"

"No, it's not about that. I think the last sentence should be clear and powerful. Are you angry with me?" I respond, "No, I'm not angry, but I am puzzled. I do think something important is transpiring between us here, but I can't quite formulate it. I'll think about it and get back to you on this."

He goes on to tell me that he wants to confront the woman he is dating and share his feelings about a matter of import, but he is ambivalent. He is torn about expressing and articulating his wishes and the nature of the disappointment. I comment, "Your wishes and requests sound reasonable to me. What is your dilemma?"

He responds, "I'm worried it won't go well. I'm worried she'll be angry." I offer, "What you are asking for seems reasonable. The energy and feelings attached to your requests may be the problem. On the one hand you are tempted to give her an ultimatum. If she doesn't agree or respond favorably, you're out of there. But, on the other hand, you are aware of the many positive features and pleasure associated with this relationship. A part of you is really not interested in ending this relationship now or in that manner. If you lead with your anxiety and anger, the conversation may not proceed as you would like." He responds, "You mean like the way I discussed the writing with you today." I recognize that he has identified something important, and I comment, "Yes, it was your anxiety and anger that captured my attention. What do you know about that?" He responds, "It's not about the writing. It's about putting my needs first and asking. I'm worried about being disappointed or not being taken seriously, and then anger becomes activated. The anger comes from another place. My fears of being disappointed perhaps. My family was not good at negotiation. I need your help with this."

The preceding vignette illustrates a relational transaction that resulted in new learning for my patient. He came to recognize both the limitations of his old form of negotiating requests and a budding sense that he might develop other more inclusive and effective ways. My patient is actively trying out and learning the relational steps involved in how one negotiates with another. "The slow transactional process of repeated relational encounters in the psychotherapeutic situation can result in increased complexity and organization in the patient's and therapist's relational procedures" (Lyons-Ruth 2004). Both patient and therapist will engage in a process that "destabilizes old forms of organization and eventually crystallizes a shift to an emergent form of procedural knowledge that is more complex and coherent" (Lyons-Ruth 2004).

In accord with infant research, therapists perceive patients' nonlinguistic cues as relational communications. Therapists provide scaffolding that fosters the patient's "ability to articulate and communicate her mental state somewhat ahead of her ability to do this herself" (Lyons-Ruth 2004).

A competent, professionally successful woman comes for treatment wanting assistance with relational dilemmas, stating, "It's hard for me to know what I want and ask for it. I expect people to know. I have difficulty putting myself first." Across time, we identify that one of the features of her dilemma is that she often does not know what she feels or what she wants. Raised in a family where she was instructed, "You're just a kid, kids don't have problems," she learned at an early age to disconnect from her inner experience. Affect and longings were countered with dissociation. At times, she is overwhelmed and confused by feeling states.

She arrives for a session after having had a "bad" business day wherein she made a computational error at work that stimulated her boss' and her criticism. As she begins to recount the facts, I notice her eyes seem full as if she might be holding back tears. I ask what she is feeling, and she focuses upon the cognitive data at hand. I listen and then restate my observation, commenting upon my perception of her facial expression: "Do you know what you're feeling?" She pauses, and I pause, and then I continue, "You look sad, as if you might cry." She responds, "I'm not sad. I don't feel sad," and continues to relate her narrative. I again bring her back to her affective state and comment: "Maybe sadness does not fit, that's my guess from the outside. However, you seem to be filled with feeling. We can study your experience and help you know more about these feelings."

Following my lead, she begins to cry. I comment, "What do you know about what you're feeling, what are you aware of?" She responds, "I feel like crying, but I do not feel sad." I encourage her to "stay with this process and see what comes up for you. We can figure this out." She sits silently, and after awhile I offer, "Maybe you feel hurt or angry at how your boss treated you?" She pauses, "I'm not sure. I don't think so." Gradually, sticking with this process, she identifies that she feels a sense of "injustice" that the way she was treated was "unfair." It reminds her of moments from her childhood when she had to take a back seat to others. The central feeling is one of unfairness. Now she sees that the feeling of being treated unfairly stimulates sadness as well.

This relational transaction and conversation with my patient opened up space for a more detailed exploration of her history, describing childhood memories of unfairness. Her dissociated feelings of anger and sadness and the deeply personal meaning she had drawn from such moments are available for exploration. Furthermore, it provided us with a template for a process of internal and interpersonal investigation of the unknown that expanded relational and affective understandings.

In the therapeutic relationship, change takes place at intersubjective moments that prompt alterations in *ways of being with* (Stern et al. 1998, p. 18). Verbal exchanges that grasp the sense of "what is happening now, here, between us" are instrumental in facilitating movement toward intersubjective understanding that is fundamental to change (Stern et al. 1998, p. 10). These moments carry a unique opportunity for expansion of self and other and states of consciousness and relatedness (Stern et al. 1998). Such moments involve feelings of unfamiliarity as they move into uncharted interpersonal territory and carry a sense of risk and possibility.

A young man joins a coed relational psychotherapy group hoping to increase his understanding of self in relationships and become his own kind of man. He engages tentatively at first, studying the group members and the leader. Does this group have something deeply personal to offer him, he wonders? How engaged will he allow himself to become? Will he allow the group to see and know parts of him that stimulate conflict and shame for him? Across time, he does allow the group to know him, including caring for him in new ways while celebrating his special qualities. The group members' warmth, respect, and abiding desire to know one another in detail provides pleasure and new interpersonal learning opportunities.

Dissatisfied with his present employment and in transition around relationships, he longs "to spread his wings" and seek new opportunities and challenges. He applies for employment in other parts of the country in spiritual communities that will afford him the opportunity to take on work he loves and continue to engage deeply with himself. As he shares his thoughts and decision-making process with the group, I begin to feel that by leaving the group at this point in time he abandons valuable developmental opportunities. The closeness and caring that he has experienced in the group is stimulating internal disequilibrium and shifting him into unfamiliar interpersonal territory. I know he is uncomfortable, but I believe this process will allow for new development. As I think about him and listen to him in the group, I sense that moving now will interrupt a valuable process for him. I decide to share my feelings and thinking with him.

I comment, "I have been thinking about you and your plans to relocate, and I would like to share my thinking and feelings with you. While I understand that this is your decision, my preference would be for you to stay in Boston and spread your wings in this group. Spreading your wings here would involve deepening your engagement with yourself and the other members who see you, know you well, and care for you. Seems to me that you are at a turning point here. Staying would allow you to experiment with new ways of being with yourself and others. On the one hand, you long to be deeply engaged with yourself and others. You do want to be known and value emotional honesty. Yet, deep engagement feels risky and stimulates feelings that are confusing and threatening. I believe you might learn more about intimacy and regulating feelings if you stay here with us." Initially startled and pleased by my comments, he exclaims "Damn! I mean in a good way. Makes me feel very cared for, and I wasn't expecting this. I'll have to think about it."

During the next several weeks, we explore and discuss exactly what this would mean for him, including why I didn't mention this earlier. I respond, "I'm sorry it took me so long to formulate this, but it has just taken form in my own mind." He wants to know what would be different if he stayed. I comment, "I don't know exactly. I am extending an invitation for you to work on deepening your relationship with yourself and others. You would be signing up for an uncharted journey. I understand this is a deeply personal choice, and you might choose not to pursue this at this time. Please do not mistake this as my belief that you must continue on this journey now or it will be lost to you. I don't believe that. But this is a moment of both being known in relationships here, and being vulnerable. I sense openness to new possibilities for you. Think about it."

With reflection and time, he decides he will remain in Boston and in the group. Excited about spreading his wings in this group, he has faith that it is the right choice for him for now. When he announces he will stay, the group is ecstatic and lets rip a cheer of delight. I imagine he senses at that moment, if not before, what a beloved member of the group he has become.

Authentic interpersonal moments lead to novel intersubjective contact that alters and leads to a newly created dyadic state specific to the participants. Patients experience and learn new ways of being and conducting themselves through nonverbal, "unconscious experience that becomes more articulated and integrated through participation in more coherent and collaborative forms of intersubjective interaction" (Lyons-Ruth 2004).

THE THERAPEUTIC RELATIONSHIP AND CONVERSATION

A crisis of attachment may mark the beginning of the therapeutic relationship, as patients are unprepared and unsettled by the feelings stimulated by emotional engagement with a therapist (Russell 1976a, 1976b, 1976c, 1976d, 1976e, 1983). If my patient successfully allows herself to know and feel her inner experience and to take me in as a potentially new relationship, she may soon experience intense feelings accompanied by a sense of longing. The activation of her feelings and wishes in the therapeutic relationship creates internal disequilibrium and crisis. Rupture of relatedness is a very real risk (Russell 1976a, 1976b, 1976d, 1976e, 1983). Acknowledging the depth of attachment and attendant feelings precipitates a crisis and propels the patient into uncharted territory. Patients are terrified of both the intense longings and aggression that may surface and of letting go or modifying their defensive self. A state of internal disequilibrium will follow, leading to an emotional opening up that allows for new growth and mastery through relational transactions and negotiations with a therapist. A caring, connected therapeutic relationship wherein a person may become known and get to know herself provides the foundation for new experience.

The evolution of the capacity to know and to feel can only take place in a relationship (Russell 1983), and "emotion in the therapeutic relationship equals opportunity for change or transformation" (Maroda 1999a, p. 34). Relying upon recent findings from mother-infant studies, Tronick et al. (1998) formulate that each individual in the therapist-patient dyad "is a self-organizing system that creates his or her own states of consciousness." These states of consciousness can be "expanded into more coherent and complex states in collaboration with another self-organizing system" (Tronick et al. 1998, p. 292). In relationships, mutual regulation of affect can give rise to new self-organization and relational procedural knowledge for both participants. In the therapist-patient dyad, much like the mother-infant dyad, our patients comprehend our complex emotional being often through nonverbal mechanisms and can sense the therapist as a person.

Through the process of surrendering to, rather than defending against, the full range of her affective experience, a patient may establish a deep emotional connection with her therapist. A safe intersubjective connection allows a patient to feel and examine costly, repetitive relational and affective scenarios that she creates in all relationships. In part, it is through the experience of intense affect and a working through of these affective and relational scenarios that patients develop new affective, self, and relational templates.

My patients often comment to me, "I don't know what I don't know. I need you to help me with this." Often, they simply cannot conjure up feelings, relational moves, or possibilities that are out of their experience. It is our task as therapists to open up space for the development of other, previously unthinkable, possibilities.

A woman begins treatment and is instantly flooded with previously unconscious deep longings and feelings. Her solution is to titrate her attachment and her affect by seeing me less often. Scheduling two appointments per month, her capacity to wall off feelings and compartmentalize her experience remains largely intact. During this time, I learn that my patient's childhood experience includes traumatic relational losses and feeling unimportant to her self-occupied mother.

After eight months of intermittent contact, a personal health crisis occurs, and the patient feels a desire to come more often. At the end of a session, the patient requests an appointment the following week on the same day. While I am unable to accommodate her request, I offer her an appointment at a time that is difficult for her. She becomes visibly agitated and angry and comments, "I've been coming on the same day for a long time, and now you don't have time for me. It feels like you don't want to see me or like you're so busy you don't have time for me anymore." I am startled by her response and comment, "I can see you're distressed. I am committed to working with you. I was simply not expecting that you would want to return next week, as that has not been your pattern. I wonder if you could see your way clear to accept this appointment for next week. We will discuss your feelings and our misunderstanding." After the session, I receive a voice-mail message expressing how hurt and angry she feels about our conversation and her strong impulse not to continue this work with me. She continues: "If I didn't have such deep respect for you and your work, if you were any other therapist, I would quit."

During the intervening time, I check my appointment book to be sure I had an accurate accounting of how often we had met during the past several months. I want to be sure that my feelings or transference had not distorted the data in my memory. We, in fact, had met infrequently, but I knew that my patient felt as if we had been in more contact. When she returns, I comment, "Your feelings about this interaction and our relationship are most important. I suggest we focus on your experience and how you made meaning of this event. I will, however, share my experience and understanding at some point so that you might understand what I was thinking and feeling as well. I want to understand how we could be on such different pages."

Flooded with sadness and grief, she shares her feeling that I did not want to know her or work with her any longer. My unavailability was a sign that she was unimportant and that she would lose me as she had tragically lost others in his life. "How many other people do I have to lose!" As we explore her feelings, I wonder if she had, in that moment, experienced me as like her mother: self-occupied and disinterested in her. Did this moment remind her of the sudden and tragic death of her partner? Or perhaps this exchange stimulated her memory of a beloved therapist she had lost in an untimely fashion? Her history and experience with tragic loss and emotional abandonment was densely layered and alive in our relationship.

She readily accepts my interpretation of her experience, as I share with her, "I know that you feel deeply connected to me and feel safe with me. We have been meeting one or two times per month, and I had no idea that you would like to alter how often we meet. During this time of crisis, you feel so vulnerable that you became convinced that I would abandon you as others had. I believe this is a memory from your childhood and resonates with other tragic losses. You don't have to lose me. I'm sure we can work out this schedule dilemma with conversation, time, and patience. Sharing your wishes and feelings with me will be helpful."

She appears relieved and ends the session weeping, saying, "I don't want to leave. This is the only place I feel safe. I'm so scared all the time." I offer comfort to her by contextualizing her severe distress as related to her medical condition that has disarmed her coping mechanisms. I reassure her that I will help her with these feelings and worries.

This moment carried a sense of risk and possibility and held the potential for altering my patient's ways of being and for rearranging her expectations for our relationship. Would we be able to negotiate these painful feelings and reach a new understanding, or would the relationship become derailed? This moment prompted an intersubjective exchange that moved us along toward new understandings about my patient and our relationship. As in this case, authentic moments lead to novel intersubjective contact that "alters and establishes a newly created dyadic state specific to the participants" (Lyons-Ruth 2000).

The power of attachment and the hope and rage associated with deep, often unconscious longings and frustration are internally disruptive, in some cases even dangerous. Our most vulnerable patients may not be able to tolerate safely the feelings stimulated by the experience of being connected and cared for. The inevitable frustration and loss that accompanies such caring in a therapeutic relationship may be unbearable. Our patients shield themselves from knowledge of such feelings for good reasons.

The following case illustrates the positive and destructive power of attachment as well as the feelings stirred by the therapeutic relationship.

During my internship twenty-plus years ago, a fifty-year-old woman with a major mental illness who had steadfastly eschewed professional help for years was referred for psychotherapy by her internist after an exacerbation of symptoms. Sarah was willing to meet with me every week although she didn't understand how it might be helpful. Frankly, I also wondered if I might have anything to offer her. She lived a desperately lonely and isolated life with her older brother, who often mistreated her. The sole positive connection in her life was Skippy, her terrier, who had been her close companion for eight years. Many therapeutic sessions focused on Skippy. I came to understand deeply how much she loved this dog and how this relationship gave her life meaning and purpose. It became clear that Skippy was the one relationship in her life that did not harm her, and through our conversations I suspected that she was allowing me to become important to her as well. Meeting with Sarah was enjoyable, and I became quite fond of her. She never missed an appointment, and while she never verbally acknowledged the depth of her attachment, I knew it and sensed how much she valued our time and my attention.

In the winter, as the imposed time limit on our relationship was approaching, Sarah developed an elaborate paranoid delusion about the impending tragic loss of her beloved companion, Skippy. Convinced that rogue neighborhood boys would kidnap and murder Skippy, she developed an equally tragic defensive shield against her sense of powerlessness and the inevitability of this loss. Her solution was to schedule Skippy's death and have him put to sleep. Horrified, I prayed that my patient would not act on these feelings and her plan.

Sarah's fears of losing Skippy were her displaced feelings about the impending loss of our relationship that she could not passively endure. I would be leaving at the end of the academic training year. There was nothing she could say or do to stop that from happening. It was true, but she didn't have to lose Skippy as well. I tried to explain this to her and help her identify and hold her feelings with no success. "Sarah, your overwhelming fears of losing Skippy may be feelings about losing our relationship. In a way, I'm being torn away from you. My leaving fills you with great sadness and anger. You don't have to lose our relationship and Skippy too. I believe Skippy is safe. Let me help you sort this out. Losing Skippy would be tragic. You need and deserve to have him in your life." My words had no effect as she had shifted states and shut me out. I felt powerless, terrified, and angry with my patient. I imagined this was an attenuated version of her feelings with me. How could she do this to herself and me?

In the late spring, Sarah informed me that she had taken Skippy to a clinic and put him to sleep. Sarah was now grief-stricken, and I was overwhelmed with a sense of grief and guilt myself. I understood Sarah's murder of Skippy as a defense against suicidal and homicidal feelings and a wish to be in control. While killing Skippy was a defensive solution to escape suicidal and homicidal rage, the loss of Skippy allowed her rage to turn into grief. Her grief became the focus of our sessions until our good-bye. The death of Skippy concretized her loss, and her displaced grief somehow seemed more manageable.

Sarah taught me about the power of deep attachment and of the intense and disruptive feelings that may accompany a deep connection with another. The therapeutic challenge of offering containment and assisting patients with symbolic expression of feelings may be daunting at times. Despite her grief and rage at my loss, Sarah's positive attachment to me made it possible for her to consider seeing another therapist after my departure. After an interval of time, she did begin with another therapist and eventually invited a puppy into her life.

Intense affect in the therapeutic relationship is a sign of an emotional opening up by the patient and often signals a defensive fluidity that opens up the possibility of change and new growth. Differentiating the therapeutic relationship from previously hurtful or abandoning connections is both healing and growth producing. A deep connection with affective attunement provides a relational context for a patient to expand transference possibilities and self-experience.

Often patients deny, disown, and simply forget more benign or even enhancing connections with historic others because this has not been the salient mode of relating, or they may do this as a defense against disappointment and anger. Both loving and hateful experiences leave internal residues and sometimes are "not integrated resulting in different, multiple versions of self with others" (Mitchell 2000, p. 23). Through the transference relationship with the therapist, the patient may reconnect with the full range of multiple versions of the self, including positive life experiences that have been forgotten.

After an intimate therapeutic conversation with a patient who is deeply conflicted about loving and being loved and is in the process of negotiating the conflict and pleasure surrounding our deep connection, the patient comments, "Your love for me has helped me tap into my positive feeling reservoir. I'm feeling and remembering other moments in my life when I felt loved and cherished. It makes me sad, but it's good." Or a patient who comes to treatment feeling injured and hated by her mother develops a close connection with me. While allowing herself to become profoundly sad about her losses and the relational sequelae of her mother's emotional abuse, she reports, "Our relationship has made me think about my mother. I'm beginning to remember moments, positive moments. Some of my mother's comments make me know that she did love me even though she didn't know how to be a good parent. Believing my mother loved me is new for me."

A SPECIAL RELATIONSHIP

Even for the seasoned therapy consumer, the therapeutic relationship and the feelings engendered may be overwhelming and profoundly unsettling. As one patient writes, "the chair seemed to tilt like a cradle, in danger of depositing me at the feet of this woman I had recently met. I was unprepared for this strong reaction" (Wolitzer 2000, p. 98). Psychotherapy patient-authors describe the range and intensity of their feelings in the treatment relationship as perverse, odd, touching, and perplexing. As one writer comments (Wolitzer 2000, p. 98), the therapeutic process transformed her to a "regressed babbling state" that simultaneously intrigued and terrified. Feeling small, childlike, pubescent, and so dependent on a therapist may be troubling and frightening. Our patients dream of us, call our answering machines to hear our voices, ruminate about the helpfulness or harmfulness of such a strong and strange connection, love us, and hate us. As patients comment to me, "I love coming here and talking to you so much, and those feelings make me feel so small." Or, "Sometimes I don't want to come, even though I know I'll leave feeling better. Do I want to know myself? Not really, I face such pain when I come here. It can be overwhelming." Or, "I hate how I feel with you. It makes me so angry with you." Or, "I feel so close to you, so connected to you. I know the feelings are real and genuine but I don't know where to place you in my mind. It's hard to create a boundary in my mind. Where does this relationship fit?"

Patients may be troubled by the intensity of the connection they feel and confused about where to place me in their internal relational grid. I'm not, and never will be a friend, a kin, or in a romantic attachment and, in fact, do not fit into any known category. Yet, my patient may experience intense feelings with and about me that remind her of other relationships or surpass any connection that she has made in the world. Part of the conundrum for a patient is that she has no model for the way to think and feel about me.

I suggest to patients that they form a new category in their mind for our relationship. Our professional relationship is a relationship: a special, deeply personal, maybe intimate, bounded relationship. It includes real feelings based on our personal qualities and particular features of our relational engagement and relational scenarios linked to the past. How I feel with and about her and how she feels with and about me will be centrally important. The structure of our relationship may allow my patient to develop and work through feeling states about self and other that would be impossible outside the office. Our work together will be a laboratory to study her feelings and the development of our relationship. Hopefully it will give us a window into how this works and does not work for her in the world. I expect we will cocreate a therapeutic relationship influenced by primary relational and affective scenarios as well as the idiosyncrasies of each of our personalities and temperamental match. Our task will be to acknowledge and honor both the real aspects of our unique connection and relationship, differentiating past feelings and scenarios from the present relational context. This may be cold comfort to my patient. The grief and disappointment around the boundaries of our relationship may be as intense and disorienting as the pleasure and excitement of feeling deeply known and deeply cared for by me.

THERAPEUTIC STANCE

The most helpful therapeutic stance assumes a collaborative, nonhierarchical, nonauthoritarian approach with our patients. Rauch (Rauch et al. 2002) describes her stance and relationship with patients as that of a copilot, and I believe that metaphor captures the essence of a truly collaborative approach. Havens' (1989) teaching about counterprojective techniques describes the most useful therapeutic stance with an image of a patient and a therapist sitting together on a bench looking out at the world together. His image captures nicely the importance of feeling that your therapist is on your side.

"We will be a team" is an important value, even though I fully understand that deep therapeutic work will involve painful passages of deep longings and injured feelings. A collaborative stance implies mutual responsibility and accountability in the therapeutic process and challenges subtly patients' wish that I will fix them. If all goes well, my patient will experience me as not on her side at moments. My task is to create a structure wherein these feelings and moments may be acknowledged and processed between us.

Consider the following example. After five years of several-times-a-week psychotherapy, in which my patient and I negotiate interpersonal safety and conflicted feelings about herself, she discloses, "I used to love you and hate you. I hated you for those moments when I felt small and disappointed. I felt you were criticizing me or judging me. Now I just feel love here. I know my self-critic that I was assigning to you shaped those other moments. Now, I just feel loved and safe knowing I can bring any feeling or dilemma here, and you will not judge me. It is okay, and we will figure it out together."

All therapeutic relationships contain a mixture of shadows from primary relationships and the development of a new, real relationship with the therapist in the present. In clinical work, the reality is that we constantly hold and consider both the transference relationship and the real relationship. A therapist who retreats behind an insistence that a particular feeling or interaction was only a manifestation of transference will likely injure and alienate her patient. Labeling a feeling as only transference has historically been a way for a therapist to protect herself, absolve her of any responsibility, and emotionally abandon her patient. Sorting out these interactions with patients requires a dyadic perspective that genuinely views these moments as cocreated.

Often, my patient responds to visible but barely discernable shifts in my affect, expression, demeanor, or the nature of my relatedness to her. She has, in fact, accurately perceived some data about me and our relationship that she imbues with deeply personal meaning based on primary relational scenarios or past moments with me. My task is to acknowledge my contribution to triggering this scenario and to assist my patient in more fully understanding her internal contribution.

A patient shares tender feelings, and my internal climate shifts as I am touched and startled by the direct expression of her feelings. Unknown to me, she notices a change in my feeling state accompanied by a shift in my facial expression. She voices her worry about whether it is okay to share these feelings with me. In the next session, she tells me, "You hurt my feelings. When I was sharing my feelings about you, your expression changed. I saw your facial expression and felt you were disgusted, recoiling from me. It was very humiliating and I felt angry after I left."

At the moment in the previous session, I knew she had accurately perceived an internal shift in my feelings. However, I felt that she interpreted this change in line with her deep-seated self-doubts about being worthy and lovable. From her early family relationships, I knew that she felt that something was wrong with her and that she was too much for anyone to hold in relationship. I comment, "Let's talk about it." She continues, "Don't tell me it's my imagination or it's about me. I saw your face." I respond, "You are so attuned to me and scan my face to detect any reaction to you. You did notice a shift in my energy level. However, you made deeply personal meaning about that shift based on your feelings about yourself. Maybe you feel critical of your close feelings with me? I wonder if you are worried about doing something to ruin the care and connection you feel with me."

Though patients re-create scenarios from the past, they also develop real feelings for us based on who we are and how we treat them. It is vital that we acknowledge both components and respect our patients' experience while assisting them in differentiating the past from the present.

Respectfully disagreeing and acknowledging separate emotional realities is a common feature of establishing a deep connection and working from within the relationship. It allows for a process of differentiation that values dialogue and difference, inviting patients to begin to experience a relationship where power is shared and submitting to another's will is not required. For patients, learning how to negotiate is a mainstay of the therapeutic process. I might highlight this process with a patient by commenting, "I know we see this differently," or "I know you have a different feeling about this." I may comment, "We may have to agree to disagree on this issue," or "May I offer another perspective here?"

An important aspect of the therapeutic relationship involves educating my patient and demystifying the therapeutic process and relationship. If patients are to allow themselves to participate fully in an intimate therapeutic relationship, they need and want to understand the point and why this will be helpful. As therapist, I need to be able to respond openly and honestly and offer my formulations. Frankly, the process of surrendering to a deep, intimate, emotional engagement with a therapist is too painful, frightening, and disruptive for patients to undertake without some understanding of how or why this may prove useful to them.

> A woman who came for treatment around a discrete life crisis is torn about continuing in treatment after the resolution of the crisis. She both knows she needs more therapeutic attention regarding her relational dilemmas and is frightened and intolerant of these feelings. I offer her the following formulation. "You have a dilemma and it's hard to confront. On the one hand you have a conflict about a deep commitment to someone you really care for and who cares for you. You need help to understand what gets in the way of your making a serious commitment to a loving relationship. You have many talents and competing interests. You are able to successfully distract yourself from this dilemma around relationships. I wonder if you are frightened about becoming deeply engaged with me. Perhaps you worry that the same feelings will be stimulated in our relationship that have been so problematic with others. It is a deeply personal decision regarding when or if to do this work. This may not be the right time; perhaps it makes sense to wait until these dilemmas get in the way of your building a happy life."

Beginning the therapeutic relationship often precipitates a crisis of attachment as the patient is filled with both hope about a new connection and enormous anxiety and uncertainty about reliving old traumas. Educating my patient about the therapeutic process and sharing my formulations about her affective, relational, and developmental edges are essential to establishing containment and inviting her full and deep participation. Patients need and want more than an empathic relationship that accurately reflects their affective state and internal dilemmas. I believe they want to deeply understand how they work internally and in relationships, as well as how I feel about them.

Patients want to know with as much specificity as possible my assessment of the therapeutic work to be done. Sharing my view of the developmental trajectory of our work, I offer them a relational frame. Hopefully this will assist them in managing moments of disequilibrium and overwhelming affect, particularly in our relationship. This information provides a cognitive structure to anchor the relationship, contain unbearable feelings, and assist them with differentiating the past from the present. I think of it as providing a cognitive relational latticework for mastery that outlines the obstacles to building a happier life.

The more information I can give my patient about how I understand his intrapsychic, interpersonal, and developmental dilemmas, the better.

A patient who is conflicted about himself and feels deeply connected to me is panicked and beset with disorganizing separation anxiety as his planned absence approaches. He is worried he will sink into a negative self-state accompanied by depression while separated from me. He depends upon my positive feelings for him to sustain a positive feeling of himself. In an effort to offer comfort, provide a cognitive grid of his internal dilemma, and increase his self-understanding, I comment, "You worry that the good you feel will stay with me and that you will be unable to carry those feelings with you. You feel good when you experience yourself with love and care by another, and you look for somebody you admire who looks favorably upon you, who loves and admires you. It allows you to feel decent about yourself. You're afraid that on your trip there won't be anybody around who loves you. It leaves you with the terror of a young child who can't yet hold onto an internal connection with a caring other. You will not be so scared of being without me when you can hold onto an internal connection with me even during separations."

Sharing this formulation affirms our connection, explains his distress in developmental terms, and outlines the work to be done. It provides him with a relational intrapsychic strategy for comforting himself while away.

My patient's strengths, innate talents, and adaptive coping strategies are therapeutic assets. I trust and expect that I will rely upon her resources and self-knowledge about what's helpful to guide the therapeutic process. As my years in clinical practice increase, I remain humbled by what I do not know and stunned by the loss of truths once held dear. Learning from my patients, I accept that often they know best what will work for them.

A woman in crisis who I had been seeing multiple times per week is now stabilized and doing well. She desires to come less often because receiving so much of my time and attention leads her to feel that something is wrong with her. I am disappointed both because I thoroughly enjoy working with her and because I sense that she would benefit greatly from a deep engagement that allows her to discover who she is and what she wants. In the conversation around altering her frequency of meetings, I comment that I wonder whether it will be possible to keep our focus on her inner experience and our relationship or whether the accounting of life events will distract us. Convinced that meeting less often is the only way for my patient to proceed, we do just that. To my surprise, meeting less often allows this woman to deepen her engagement with our relationship and herself. She uses our time to study her feelings of unworthiness and self-contempt as she forges ahead with developing new relationships. I surmise that meeting once a week is the optimal distance for this woman at this point in time. In part this schedule works because it diminishes her self-contempt and intolerance around needing and wanting my time and attention. My patient knew exactly what she needed at this point in time.

I accept fully that I will commit many mistakes and injure patients by not being helpful at times. When stimulated by my own internal process or transference, I will emotionally leave or dominate the relationship. It is to be expected. Sometimes, particularly if my patient knows me well, she may sense my mounting tension or a build-up of affect. She offers comments that I have employed with her at another moment, which aim to assist me in regulating my affect. For example, a patient may comment, "Stay with me," or "You're reacting before I've finished." Often, my patient has read me well, and such comments assist me in regulating my affect, putting myself on pause, heightening my self-monitoring.

Consider the following example illustrating my injuring a patient. A patient who struggles to identify his wishes and ask for what he needs is describing a recent cycle of disconnection from himself. I respond with, "This system ensures that you will have little chance of figuring out what you need." My patient looks stunned, pauses, and responds, "Comments like that are not helpful." His words draw my attention to my feelings and intent around this comment. I realize my tone of voice was provocative and playful, but clearly not helpful. I wonder if he thought I was mocking him. I respond, "Thank you for saying that so directly. Clearly, that comment was insensitive, maybe rude. I'll think about why I chose to say that and in that manner. Can you tell me what you feel and specifically how that comment was unhelpful?" After a discussion of how his feelings were injured, I comment, "I'm sorry I hurt your feelings. I'm pleased you noticed and were able to tell me." Through this conversation, I realized that during my patient's opening discussion of this material, I felt as if he had moved away from the therapeutic relationship and was distancing himself. Frustration and a feeling of distance between us stimulated my comment and led to a conversation about the vicissitudes of connection and disconnection between us.

Surprisingly, my error and insensitivity do not unduly alarm my patient. Through ongoing dialogue he reveals to me how meaningful and reassuring it is to him that I both make mistakes and assume responsibility, commenting, "That's why I trust you and feel so safe with you."

Hopefully, the treatment frame and therapeutic stance will allow me to study these moments with my patient when they occur. My aim is to fully understand the feelings involved and what is being re-created by each of us. These moments add to the patient's self-awareness and understanding and introduce the reality that I make mistakes. Acknowledging and accepting full responsibility for my contribution opens up space for intimate dialogue and the possibility of the patient developing a more compassionate and caring self-stance. It challenges the notion that the patient is damaged and I am perfect, paving the way for new perspectives on self and relationships.

A therapeutic stance that emphasizes humility and emotional honesty with regard to the therapeutic relationship facilitates the development of trust and psychological safety. Patients are often ashamed and deeply conflicted about who they are and wrestle with harsh self-critics or an internalized denigrated view of self. A therapist who is willing to be visible and emotionally known in the therapeutic process leaves patients feeling respected.

THERAPIST'S SELF-MONITORING

Creating a safe place for the unfolding of the therapeutic relationship involves the therapist's willingness to examine her self-interest and influence on the therapeutic process. Therapeutic work may be both deeply gratifying and destabilizing for the therapist as well as the patient. A therapist's self-care and attention to her inner affective experience and points of identification are vital to maintaining her equilibrium and sorting out projective identifications. Casement's (1991) concept of internal supervision is most helpful here. Internal supervision may provide "a counterbalance to the many pressures upon a therapist in session (Casement 1991, p. 30). A compassionate and clinically curious stance regarding deeply personal feelings toward patients both informs the therapeutic work and increases self-awareness. Any of my feelings captures my supervisory attention. If we are to gather in and hold dissociated affects and self-fragments from our patients, any feeling, sensation, or thought is of clinical interest.

Personal therapy and consultation are essential components of professional self-care and play a vital role in assisting therapists with managing complicated feelings with patients. For the most part, the experienced clinician can do this on her own, but needs to know when to get help. Clinicians at every level of practice need forums to routinely discuss and share their work with patients (Gabbard 2000; B. Pizer 2000; S. A. Pizer 2000).

It is not easy, but it is essential for therapists to self-monitor and explore their identification with their patients. As therapists, we are also vulnerable to defending against or distracting ourselves from affects or relational scenarios that produce pleasure or discomfort. Without access to

and acceptance of our inner experience, these feelings may unconsciously influence our clinical choices or become behavioral enactments.

Our best hope is to identify and contain these feelings and make therapeutic meaning. For example, at the end of a session with a long-term
patient with major mental illness, I catch myself as I almost comment,
"See you next week, sweet pea." "Sweet pea" is an affectionate mothering
phrase I have used with my children. The fantasy of saying this to my patient alerts me to the depth of my connection and the intensity of my maternal feelings with this woman. I am not sure if she shares this feeling
with me. While speaking with another patient on the phone who is out of
town, I find myself flooded with sadness. I struggle to understand if the
feeling is born out on my patient's missing me or my missing my patient.
Perhaps it signals some complex identification process between us, I
wonder. Or finding myself aroused and drawn to a patient, I fantasize
about how I feel and who this patient reminds me of and imagine how my
patient may feel with me. A self-scrutinizing and clinically curious stance
allows me to monitor my feelings and connection and assess how to understand and therapeutically employ this data. As therapists, if we are
open to ourselves and emotionally vulnerable with our patients, we will
be poised on an intimate edge, managing intense feeling states and self
and other boundaries.

Without careful attention to our inner process, intense affect, and
points of identification, we may use our patients for our own purposes,
often unconsciously. Influenced by conscious or unconscious identification, we may replicate aspects of our personal treatment experience with
our patients. Graduate and professional training often neglects to teach
therapists the clinical and protective value of self-care. In worst-case
training scenarios, therapists feel overly burdened and not allowed to take
reasonable care of themselves secondary to demanding on-call schedules
and patient caseloads.

Creating a sustaining life structure with a reasonable balance between
therapeutic work and leisure and recreational time is essential to maintaining one's therapeutic balance with patients. A therapist needs pleasure and loving, sustaining connections in her personal life. Without such
connections, the temptation and lure of turning to one's patients for

deeply personal needs may be more than a person can resist. Even with a sustaining life structure, any one of us may become so vulnerable during times of personal crisis, illness, or loss that we look to our patients to satisfy personal needs. A therapist must take good care of herself, including supervision and consultation, if she is to be available to take good care of her patients.

USE OF AUTHORITY AND THERAPEUTIC AGGRESSION

While I favor a collaborative approach and emphasize mutuality, I firmly believe the therapist is the paid expert and must assume overall responsibility and accountability for the therapeutic process. Valuing mutuality and a collaborative approach does not relieve the therapist of this responsibility. The therapist's use of her authority and aggression in the therapeutic process are essential features. Modell (1990), a respected analyst and teacher, shared the following story. His nine-year-old son wanted to see the newly released *Jaws* movie and engaged in a persuasive campaign to convince his dad. Though Modell worried that this film was too frightening for his young son and shared his concerns with him, the boy persisted in trying to win over his father. After several rounds of father and son each sharing his perspective, Modell agreed to accompany his son to the movie. After the movie, his son is terrorized and comments to his dad, "Why did you take me to that movie? It was much too scary for a nine-year-old boy. I'll be afraid to go swimming now." Modell commented that he was worried that his son would be frightened and that's why he didn't want him to see this movie: "I tried to talk with you about my worries." To which the boy comments, "Dad, you didn't say it loud enough." As a therapist, I mindfully strive to speak "loud enough," so that my patient will hear me knowing full well that she might choose to view the movie regardless. We will manage the affective and relational sequelae of the movie together. Often, one simply cannot avoid a "*Jaws* experience," and valuable developmental possibilities arise out of these moments.

Dominated by self-distortions and transference schemas, and blind to their effects on others, patients need our assistance with feelings and dilemmas that they cannot see. Although patients are vulnerable and worried about being hurt, my experience is that patients do want and need our perspective, even though it creates a sense of internal disequilibrium.

There are moments when a relational approach including a perspective from the other is most valuable. Exclusively focusing on patients' self-development neglects valuable relational and affective growth and learning. Offering an outside perspective, of course, works best when a therapist has established a mutually trusting, emotionally honest relationship with her patient. Without a sense of mutual trust and emotional vulnerability between therapist and patient, an outside perspective may simply be experienced as injurious.

During a recent conversation with a colleague debating the use of therapeutic aggression and a relational approach, my colleague comments, "I'm reluctant to share any negative feelings with my patients or an outside perspective. When I was in treatment, my analyst shared an outside perspective about me that I thought was inaccurate and insulting. It hurt my feelings and wasn't useful. I still remember how it felt." My colleague is, of course, highlighting the risks associated with such interventions but also the long-lasting influence of our personal treatments. If we have no models to emulate, we may avoid the daunting task of offering therapeutically valuable but discrepant data to our patients.

I believe many therapists avoid what they imagine will be a difficult conversation about a patient's behavior, feelings, or the therapeutic relationship, ostensibly out of a fear of injuring the patient. I also wonder if these therapists fear the patient's anger directed back at them. Clearly, as a therapist, I do try to offer comments in the most palatable form for my particular patient. But the reality is that an interpretation or an outside perspective that stimulates you to view parts of yourself that you loathe or find unacceptable hurts. I believe such injuries and disappointments are an inevitable part of the therapeutic process and relationship. To imagine or to teach our patients that intimate connections may be devoid of difference, disappointment, or conflict is not helpful and does not represent my view of human relationships.

In these moments, therapists may fear their own internal affective states. Therapists' fears of causing injury or worries of inflicting their feelings upon their patients may point to an intense but unacknowledged identification with their patient around a particular affective state. The decision to not deeply engage with a patient in those moments is likely to serve as protection for the therapist under the guise of protecting the patient.

A depressed woman comes for treatment of her childhood abuse, "self-sabotaging tendencies," and low self-esteem. She would like relief from her anguish but is reluctant to become deeply engaged with me. She worries that feelings of dependency and anger will be stimulated by our relationship. She painstakingly regulates her surrender to herself and to me. During many years, a trustworthy, caring, connection grows. As the safety in the therapeutic relationship deepens, the patient becomes increasingly vulnerable to herself and open with me about her sense of aloneness in the world. While she now knows she is profoundly lonely, socially isolated, and sad, she cannot imagine a suitable partner. Although she denies this, I wonder if the major obstacle is her deep sense of unworthiness and fear that no one would want her.

Now she allows me to care actively and visibly for her and counts on our connection to comfort and soothe herself. Beset by a life-threatening medical condition and overwhelmed by the sudden death of an abusive family member, my patient is about to embark on a trip "home" that portends to be emotionally dangerous. After much discussion, I invite her to borrow an object from my office while on this trip. I imagine this token will help to keep alive our connection, help soothe her, and remind her that she has separated from her family. Pleased and comforted by my gesture, she asks me to choose an item for her, which I do.

When she returns from her trip, she does not return the object from my office. Curious and puzzled, I wait to see how and when she will raise this issue with me. She never does. There is no mention of the borrowed object. Furthermore I do not hear any symbolic references to this material in our sessions. What to do? Out of a sense of powerlessness, I begin to question the wisdom of my decision to loan an object. I would not be in this quandary if I had not made such an offer. Fleetingly annoyed with my patient and myself, I struggle to imagine how we might have a conversation about this that would be useful. I shift my attention to my patient and our relational history. I fantasize about her feelings about this object, and I imagine she has emotionally split-off her feelings about the object as she often has about our relationship. I wonder if her keeping this object is a signal about the depth of her hunger and loneliness that she cannot bear to experience. I consider the possibility that feeling so cared for stimulates anger with me for tempting her with feelings that she cannot yet replicate in the world outside my office.

I am worried and anxious but resolved about raising this issue with my patient. At the beginning of a session, I comment, "I've been thinking about the carved figurine I lent you from my office. I am interested in what your internal process has been, how you've been thinking and feeling about it and our relationship." My patient looks startled and comments, "I was supposed to give that back to you?" as if this is new information. I comment, "I am interested in your memory and your understanding of how we negotiated this." My patient responds, "I have only a vague memory. I don't remember." I comment, "As I recall the conversation, I remember sharing with you my thinking and feelings about why I chose this object for you as well as discussing that the object was on loan and expected to be returned to me. I have wondered what became of it, but I thought you would let me know." My patient explains, "I thought you were giving me an object that you didn't like or care about. It never occurred to me that you would loan me something that mattered to you, that you would trust me with a valuable item. What if I lost it?" I respond, "It's hard for you to imagine I would value and trust you with something important to me. I believe you thought I was loaning you an item I didn't care about because it's so hard to trust that I care about you. I loaned you a cherished object, and I trusted you would care for it. Maybe part of you wished I was giving you this object so that it might remind you of my care for you and our connection." My patient comments, "I placed the figurine on an altar with my statues of Buddha. Each morning when I meditate I sit in front of this altar. It feels silly, but maybe it does remind me of you." I comment, "I wonder if you feel so conflicted about feeling close to me that you try to keep it out of your awareness or diminish its value like you did with the figurine."

Touched by my willingness to declare my feelings for her and loan her something of value, my patient begins to more fully discuss her feeling unacceptable and unlovable. She wishes to have more connections in her life. We were able to structure a process that allowed for an intimate conversation about the depth of care and connection in our relationship and that outlined the internal dilemma and relational edge for my patient.

It is easy to understand that a therapist might be hesitant to raise such an event with a patient. She worries about her own feelings of annoyance or about stimulating the patient's self-criticism. While there are always risks involved in deep conversations with patients that teeter on an intimate edge, there also are great developmental and therapeutic gains possible, as well.

In the previous vignette, the patient needed to behaviorally enact her devalued self-state and conflicts concerning our relationship before it could become conscious and available for discussion. The loaned object concretized the affective and relational conflicts and in a paradoxical fashion made it even more possible to examine them. To ignore or avoid discussion of such processes with patients is to remove yourself emotionally from the relationship. Hiding negative feelings feels counterproductive. Our task at these moments is to be emotionally honest and vulnerable with our patients and ourselves. Structuring a process that allows for the full range of affective and relational experience advances therapeutic dialogue. It requires that we have an abiding faith in the process and perhaps a certain amount of trust in our patients and ourselves to bear the uncertainty involved in exploring an uncharted course.

Through enactment and projective identification, our patients will invite us to injure and retraumatize them in keeping with primary relational and affective schemas. Therapists must be strong enough to hold unwanted, often nonverbal affects with patients and to resist the invitation to emotionally desert and injure our patients by abandoning our authority and participating in a process that is harmful.

A man who as a child was sexually abused by his stepbrother comes for treatment requesting help with his depression and anger. He describes several previous unhelpful treatment experiences. One involved repetitive nonsexual boundary violations within an eroticized relationship with a female therapist. This treatment left the patient enraged and confused about himself. As he begins to introduce himself, he informs me that he is terrified of another destructive treatment relationship. He was skeptical about my capacity to be of help to him and about his own capacity to change.

He meets with me twice a week, and despite his reservations, across time he engages deeply and allows me to care for him. I assist him with sorting out his intense and complex feeling states and with disentangling difficulties in other relationships. Valuing my opinion, he uses my positive regard to counter his self-criticism and contempt. I also imagine that he has protected me from the full force of his longings and disappointments. While we don't speak of it much, I sense how much he appreciates my care and attention. I, too, feel that our relationship and work has been a great help to him.

Several years into the treatment, he tells me that he wants to join a small organization in the community that I also belong to. When he shares this with me at first, I am stunned. I want to believe that when he knows I belong to that organization he will join a different chapter of this organization. Or perhaps he might identify another organization that would suit his interests. I inform him, "Did you know that I belong to that organization and actively participate?" He shares, "I didn't know you belong, but it's fine with me." He continues telling me why he has chosen this organization, and I realize he is drawn to the organization for many of the reasons that appeal to me. Of course, there is also the added dimension that his therapist will be there too. He persists with his desire to join.

I am uncomfortable and filled with a feeling of dread, worrying that this conversation will not go well. What are the relational issues being negotiated within my patient and between us? What scenarios are activated and shifting to the forefront here? What role am I being inducted into? Despite my best efforts to open up internal and relational space for inquiry, my patient is out of touch with any feelings or wishes. Any conflicts symbolically expressed by his desire to join an organization that I belong to are unavailable for inquiry.

Formulating possibilities, I wonder with my patient, "Perhaps you desire to know more about me, but it's been difficult to allow yourself to be curious because of the longing and conflict it stirs. I wonder if the desire to join this organization is a wish to be closer to me. Maybe you want to know what I feel and think about you. Would I want you in my organization?" My patient thinks about this: "I just want to join this organization. I like the mission, and I would have the opportunity to meet new people." I continue, "I do know that, but it would also affect our relationship and your treatment—maybe in a negative way. Is it hard for you to imagine that scenario?" He replies, "I don't understand what you're talking about." I continue, "Well, for instance, I wonder if sharing other relationships with me will be hard on you. I wonder if it will lead you to compare yourself to others and be harsh with yourself. In this organization, I will simply be another participant, not your therapist. I imagine there might be moments that disappoint you or hurt your feelings." My patient responds, "I don't think it will be a problem."

Through this process, I shifted through a series of self-other configurations and wide-ranging affect. Was this my problem? Perhaps I was too inflexible? Would another therapist be able to negotiate this and protect the treatment? At moments, I was flooded with anger and felt as if my patient were bullying me and trying to provoke me. I wondered if that was his experience of me and maybe explained the depth of his anger. Was he nonverbally re-creating a relational scenario around use and abuse of power? Could our difference be negotiated, or would he simply experience my decision as a violation instead of protective of him and our relationship? At other times, I mused about the dissociated longing this dilemma might embody and felt sad and sorry that we were wordless around this aspect of the experience.

I let him know that I do not believe this will work for his psychotherapy or for me. My patient is enraged. "This isn't about me. I can manage being in the same place as you. This is about you." I acknowledge this touches on an issue of privacy and comment, "Perhaps you could view my need for personal privacy as a personal handicap, a limitation if you like. It is part of who I am and how I work therapeutically. In order to be fully present and available to the treatment relationship and to respect your psychotherapy, I need to attend to my personal needs for privacy."

Now I am filled with a growing conviction that this is not a good idea for my patient, for his treatment, and for me. But I know he views this differently. His inability to consider other spaces that he might occupy heightens my worry. I feel he has dissociated other aspects of himself and cannot bear to go there. I interpret this as a signal that something nonverbal is being negotiated and enacted between us.

I inform my patient, "I cannot see my way clear to be your therapist and coparticipant in this organization. I understand that you feel it is possible for you. I may be wrong, but I don't believe it will be useful for your psychotherapy. I know you see this differently, and we may have to agree to disagree about this matter. Perhaps some therapists could see their way clear to do this. I can't do it. You have a choice here, a deeply personal choice. If you join this organization, I will not be able to continue as your therapist and will terminate our psychotherapy relationship. I will, of course, assist you in finding another therapist if you wish."

Although disagreeing with my decision, across time my patient acknowledged the value of being enraged at me without the destruction or denigration of either of us. Negotiating these intense feeling states and sense of betrayal while remaining in connection was new for my patient. Through the process of sustained inquiry and dialogue, my patient came to understand emotionally that I was not trying to hurt him. This understanding allowed him to hold his complex feeling states and begin to understand another's perspective. It differentiated our relationship from past scenarios.

Although angry and feeling betrayed, my patient decided to remain in treatment to understand his feelings and experience. Despite this injury, he felt this relationship had been of great value to him and our work was not finished. My declaration of an unambivalent decision that set a boundary around contact allowed my patient to relive, not merely remember, his problematic past in relationship with me. My patient was now more willing to engage in the exploration of his deep sense of injury and rage. The focus of exploration involved the patient's new understanding of his rage and sadism toward himself and others. This was related to his childhood abuse and identification with his stepbrother. In retrospect, this patient needed to experience me as failing him and betraying him to open access to his traumatic relational past and allow the possibility of new relational experience.

The formulation and implementation of this difficult intervention required that I maintain my outside perspective. Articulating it strongly and compassionately, I did not collude with what I believed would be a potentially harmful process. Such clinical moments stress therapists and require that they fully occupy their authority, even though it may be at odds with the patient and sometimes even other clinicians. Often the outcome is uncertain. In this case, the disequilibrium caused by asserting my authority led to developmental growth and expanded relational procedural knowledge for this man.

With patience and sensitive attention to the slow, idiosyncratic process of fitting together, the therapist and patient may develop a bounded intimate relationship that holds the promise of relational change. While the feelings stimulated by deep engagement may be gratifying and destabilizing for both therapist and patient to identify and bear, such experiences hold the seeds of transforming relational and affective experiences. The reliving of relational scenarios in a close, caring therapeutic relationship where both parties are emotionally engaged and vulnerable and open to mutual influence is developmentally valuable. In a relational matrix, expanding affective consciousness and the process of being seen reorders internal organization. New ways of feeling and being with self and other (Fonagy et al. 2002; Lyons-Ruth 1999, 2000, 2004; Maroda 1999a, 1999b; Sander 2002).

The therapist's capacity to be fully present, remain fluid and assume responsibility for her feelings and thoughts is the mainstay of therapeutic practice. While relying upon mutuality in the therapeutic process, and ultimately to be the guardian of the process is developmentally valuable. In the therapeutic relationship, we explore past residues of both "good" and "bad" experiences, identifying how they coexist and enrich present experience and relatedness (Mitchell 2000). Through nonverbal means and verbal interactions, we actively move our patients along developmentally. These nonverbal processes and interpersonal interactions provide experience and new skills for how one conducts oneself in a close collaborative relationship. These experiences bring the patient to expanded procedural knowledge, including greater contact with the self and altered ways of being with others. The therapist's capacity to exercise therapeutic authority is essential at times and necessary to protect the patient and the process.

3

STARTLING AFFECT
AND RELATIONAL
FORMULATION
OF EXPERIENCE

The power of intense and unwanted affect to disorient and derail a therapist and the treatment process may not be overstated. Startling feelings in therapeutic relationships frequently threaten to disrupt the therapeutic process or the treatment relationship by pulling the therapist out of role. As therapists, we are all vulnerable to the effects of destabilizing affects or the tug of multiple, unconscious identifications with particular patients that may threaten the therapeutic process. After each session with a new female patient, I am flooded with sexual feelings and energy, struggling with a state of arousal that is at once deeply disturbing and pleasing. The intensity of the feelings and the associated anxiety startle me, in part because I do not yet know this woman, and I am not yet sure what piece of this experience is projected from my patient and what piece comes from me. Vulnerable and uncertain, I struggle consciously to decipher the meaning and keep my therapeutic balance.

When I present this case to a colleague, he comments, "Why would you continue to see this patient? I'd refer this patient to someone else." I believe my colleague senses the potential danger and the therapeutic challenge of negotiating safely such feeling states in myself and with my patient. When confronted by overwhelming, often unwanted affect, therapists run the risk of destructive behavioral enactments or, alternatively, withdrawing from the patient and the clinical encounter. Personally, my colleague would not sign up to conduct a psychotherapy that involved such intense and unsettling personal feelings. It is not his therapeutic style or strength. Allowing ourselves to be employed by our patients in their unconscious relational project is difficult but fundamental to intrapsychic and relational change. Hanging in there, bearing intense destabilizing affect, and tolerating the unknown while formulating affective and relational meaning for both the patient and the therapist is challenging for every therapist.

While the intensity of any affect may be arousing and destabilizing for a particular therapeutic dyad, sexual and aggressive feelings are affects that unsettle and disorient therapists with some regularity. Such feelings in treatment relationships frighten therapists, stimulating shame and guilt. This hampers the therapist's capacity to formulate and employ these feelings to deepen and advance therapeutic understanding. The understanding and management of anger and aggressive feelings has historically received attention in the literature. Sexual and loving feelings have only recently been a focus of professional inquiry and reporting. While I will address both feelings in this chapter, sexual and loving feelings will receive more of my attention because I believe less attention has been paid to these feeling states.

Unrecognized, misunderstood, or inappropriately handled, startling feelings in psychotherapy may lead to a variety of unintended and untherapeutic outcomes. A young man who developed erotic feelings for his therapist relocated and is seeking further treatment. As he meets with his prospective therapist, he shares his treatment history, including the development of his sexual feelings toward his previous therapist. I surmise his new therapist was startled by this information, as she responded, "I am not an expert on erotic transferences, and if you develop sexual feelings for me I will terminate the treatment." The patient called seeking a referral to a therapist who could tolerate the emergence of erotic states in therapeutic relationships. Unintended outcomes in response to such feelings in the countertransference include therapeutic impasses, shame and isolation, and therapists' withdrawal or over-investment in the treatment process.

SEXUAL FEELINGS AND ATTRACTION

As therapists, we bring a deeply personal version of ourselves to our patients, but the depth and development of certain feeling states is inevitably shaped by the professional context (Mitchell 2000). In the consulting room, I feel panicked, passionate, hopeless, angry, and loving with patients. In each case, these feeling are based on the unique qualities of the patient, our relationship, and transference/countertransference feelings being negotiated. Gabbard (1993) prefers to conceptualize such feeling states as displaced and composed of "a mixture of a real relationship and remnants from a past object relationship" (p. 172).

Therapeutic responsibility requires a certain discipline that inhibits and forecloses the uncharted development of certain feeling states for the therapist, such as love and hate. Mitchell (2000) reminds us we chose the persons we love and hate for complex conscious and unconscious reasons. Our task as therapists is to deeply engage with our patients around understanding the dense and multiple, conscious and unconscious, motivating forces in the development of these complex states.

Mitchell (2000) believes the development of passion in the therapist is necessarily constricted by the ever-present preconscious awareness of the context and the therapist's responsibility. In addition to contextual factors, there are personal factors that facilitate or inhibit the development of these feeling states in the therapist. Personal comfort, culture, temperament, training, and a therapist's life stage may be shaping influences determining whether a therapist is more or less able to immerse herself deeply in her patient's experience around intense feeling states.

Obviously not all therapists are capable of holding onto the shaping influence of the context and the primacy of the therapists' responsibility. The incidence of professional sexual misconduct speaks to therapists' difficulty in staying connected to the version of the self that is the guardian of the process and is committed to keeping the relationship therapeutic.

All disciplines outlaw sexual contact with current patients and either prohibit or outline mandatory waiting periods for sexual contact with former patients. Some states allow malpractice suits for sex with a former patient, prohibiting sexual contact from six months to two years after therapy ends (Appelbaum and Jorgenson 1991). With regard to post-termination relationships with patients, I agree with Laura Brown (1994) that "transference has the half-life of uranium." We won't live long enough to diminish the power differential that was established with our patients in the consulting room.

Life is filled with many unexpected turns in the road and personal tragedies. We all know how difficult it is to find a therapist whom we admire and trust, and who, in fact, has been helpful. Transference feelings remain alive long after mandatory waiting periods. The longer I practice, I recognize many patients return to do a piece of work with me years later. So, my personal policy is once a patient of mine, always a patient of mine. I do not engage in social relationships or become friends with former patients. Even if my patient wishes otherwise, I save myself in the role of therapist, as I believe my patient may return years later.

Therapists who find themselves immersed in passionate loving states toward patients strive to employ these feeling states to facilitate the patient's self-understanding and personal growth. When overwhelmed by such feelings, therapists are urged to seek consultations from senior mentors, explicitly describing their personal and clinical predicament. Often, an outside perspective for the therapist proves invaluable and is of great comfort. If necessary, termination and transfer is always a possibility, although in my experience rarely necessary. With support and technical assistance, most therapists regain their equilibrium and arrive at formulations that increase their understanding of their patient, themselves, and the complex dynamic relational process. Personal treatment as well as supervision may be necessary to assist the therapist in containing and understanding her personal process and protecting the treatment.

VARIED MEANINGS OF SEXUAL FEELINGS

Patients' experiences of sexual feelings and behavior toward therapists represent and communicate a wide range of affective experiences, developmental difficulties, and interpersonal conflicts and needs. Sexuality may be a symbolic marker, distraction, or disguise for numerous other affects and phenomena. Some of the more common are need for nurturing, admiration, or soothing; avoidance of intimacy or grief; denial of dependency or passivity; and reenactment of traumatic object relations. These are not mutually exclusive categories and often cluster together. Transference love may defend against the expression of other intense and objectionable feelings in the therapeutic relationship, such as disappointment, hostility, or critical feelings.

I expect I will experience and hold sexual feelings for any and all of my patients based upon what issues they are negotiating, not upon their sexual identity or mine. Internalized homophobia sometimes prevents therapists from holding the erotic in same-sexed treatment dyads. The therapists' self-scrutiny and careful attention to the unique factors in each treatment dyad and process leads to the development of psychodynamic relational formulations.

Therapists need to consider the possible varied meanings of feelings in the treatment relationship. Sexual feelings may be a defense against the transference, a developmental milestone, or a manifestation of a treatment impasse. Erotic longings may signal a transference or countertransference impasse, a manifestation of the therapist's or the patient's resistance to taking the next step in the treatment process. Or sexual feelings may declare feelings of identification and a shared sense of longings, a validation and echoing of one's experience.

THERAPIST'S DISCLOSURE OF LOVE AND SEXUAL FEELINGS

Therapists recognize the transforming value of "therapeutic love" or "analytic love" in treatment relationships, a deep abiding care and concern for another's growth and development. Therapeutic love involves sponsoring another's development and being guardian of the process. I often wonder and worry if I never develop such feelings with or for a patient. The absence of these feelings may be very telling, revealing data about my patient's sense of self and my attachment to her. Often, other feeling states dominate the relationship.

The experience of therapeutic love in the treatment relationship may feel new and dangerous for patients. Re-creating or developing anew the early childhood experience of a deep loving attachment may stimulate sensual and sexual elements while opening up new relational possibilities for both patients and therapists. Mirroring the parent-infant relationship, this deep loving connection contains sensual, tactile, even erotic long-ings. A patient may have difficulty holding and making meaning out of the intensity of desire and the multifaceted dimensions of this deep con-nection and loving state.

For patients, the interpersonal intrapsychic journey to feeling deeply known and cared for may require traversing a foreign subjective land-scape fraught with danger and dead ends. Allowing oneself to love and be loved by a therapist often signals a separation from old self-organization and structures. This separation allows a patient the freedom to make new meaning about self and other. I hope my patient will grow to feel deeply known and emotionally held by me and will be able to hold herself in such regard. Such feelings and self-states often correlate with more alive-ness, vibrancy, fullness of feelings, and rich and varied engagement in the world.

Consideration of if and when to name, examine, and explore these feelings with my patient occupies my attention as I imagine the language, tone, and timing of such conversations. Often, my patient needs my ac-knowledgment and affirmation of her love or the deep mutual feelings of closeness and connectedness to allow herself to fully inhabit these feeling states in herself and in our relationship. These feelings may benefit from verbal acknowledgment, including full examination of the multiple and varied meanings. Or they may flourish with verbal neglect informed by a deep mutual acceptance of these nonverbal states. It depends.

Declarations of love and deep caring for one's patients require a com-plex, multilayered understanding of the intrapsychic relational meaning and anticipated effect on both patient and therapist. As a therapist, I struggle to fully understand whom my patient represents for me and to process other aspects of the transference/countertransference as well.

While I often feel loving toward my patients and routinely name and acknowledge these feelings, I am reluctant to declare, "I love you." I worry such declarations may be confusing for my patient or that she will misunderstand my intent and purpose. In some ways, the first-person use of the "L-word" obscures rather than expands and elaborates the dense layers of the self and other experience and feelings in our relationship. I carefully frame my use of the word *love,* employing the third person or a passive tense. Rather than a declaration of love, my intent is to name a feeling and relational state that I sense is in the room, residing in both my patient and me. So, for example, I might comment, "You have felt deeply known and loved in our relationship." "The feelings of love in our relationship provide you both comfort and hope." Or, "Feeling so loved stimulates anxiety and conflict for you." However, many deeply personal, even intimate, conversations detailing the nature of the therapeutic relationship and connection, while loving, do not include use of the word *love.*

In consultations, therapists who have declared their love to patients explain the rationale underlying such disclosures, commenting, "I know how much it meant to me when my therapist told me that he loved me." I often wonder if such declarations signal the therapist's desire to be "loved" or to be special or to be like her own therapist. My intent in having my patient know my subjective experience in our relationship is to expand and explore new experience, including some aspect of the self. I hope she will come to understand that the deeply personal and caring feelings emerging in our relationship also belong to her and her capacities.

For some patients the conflict around the experience of self as sexual subject or self as the object of another's desire becomes an important developmental therapeutic focus. Conflicts about self, sex, desire, aggression, self-other boundaries, and the nature of intimacy often involve therapeutic work on the erotic, immersing the therapist-patient relationship in these states. I notice when I feel drawn to a patient, often the patient knows that, particularly if my experience of those particular affects and sensations are vitally important to my patient's experience of herself and our relationship. Often, it does not require conversation; it simply is and is mutually felt and held nonverbally. Or in other cases, the feelings may be explored with a focus on the complexity of meaning to my patient and with regard to our relationship.

Our challenge is to experience and hold the erotic with our patients and ourselves in order to expand our patients' experience and understanding of self and relationships. I suggest a therapeutic stance that includes openness and availability to experience fully and understand the erotic dimension of self and other with patients. But it is hard for me to imagine a therapeutic moment or situation in which I believe a therapist's disclosure of sexual feelings or fantasies would be a useful intervention.

A therapist who remains open to the possibility of both expression and restraint around revelation of personal feelings employs disclosure differentially to deepen the therapeutic conversation and relationship. A therapist must consider how such expression may expand some therapeutic avenues, deepen access to particular self-states and affects, and foreclose the experience of others. A scrutinizing stance regarding our feelings and areas of vulnerability is valuable and protective. The guiding parameter is the therapist's mindful consideration of where she is hoping to move the therapeutic relationship and conversation with such an intervention.

FORMULATING AND HOLDING SEXUAL FEELINGS

For all patients and therapists, sexuality and sexual feelings are complicated areas of life. Therapists' capacity to fully occupy erotic countertransference, while essential, may feel dangerous (Bridges 1994; Cooper 2003; Davies 1994a, 1994b, 1998, 2003; Elise 1991; Tansey 1994). Worries about using our patients for our own pleasure or purposes, as well as our resistance to reliving some feeling aspect of our own sexual relational histories, become obstacles to freely participating in our patients' compelling enactments.

While a therapist's surrender to her own emotional experience around sexual feelings is enormously valuable, it is fraught with difficulty. The capacity to hold our patient's nonverbal but powerful experience and to manage our intense transference to such while remaining firmly planted in the role of therapist is challenging. Clinical curiosity evaporates when therapists are startled, leading to a return to concrete thinking. This hampers the creative use of the therapeutic self and forecloses deep affective understanding.

Anxiety, shame, and guilt may become obstacles to receiving our patient's nonverbal affective experience and "tumbling into another's psychic world" (Orbach 2000, p. 120). Full participation in this process involves feelings of exposure, destabilizing affects, and rapidly shifting configurations of self and other. It is a dynamic process shaped by the therapist's willingness to tolerate the emergence of her feelings, points of identification, and memories in the service of new relational experience and repair. The belief that this inchoate, uncharted journey will reveal invaluable data about our patient's self-states, inner conflicts, and developmental dilemmas guides us. This view allows us to relinquish conscious control of our inner process and be an observer of self and other. It is through this entry into the patient's inner subjective experience and being open to assigned roles that a therapist feels enough and knows enough to be able to formulate the intrapsychic and interpersonal scenarios.

Therapists consciously try to follow subtle shifts in affect, fantasies, and self-states as sensitive clues to inform and deepen the work "by sinking but not drowning in the sexualized countertransference" (Gorkin 1987, p. 105). In the case in which I was flooded with sexual feelings after each session, I had difficulty allowing myself to be open to my experience and my patient's experience. In fits and starts I tried to go with the flow and just be, but inevitably I would resort to a kind of internal wrestling with myself.

Jacobs (2002) speaks of the dynamic interweaving of the patient's transference and the therapist's countertransference in the relational context during enactments. Our task at these times is to allow ourselves to live in it, to play with it in order to process these nonverbal experiences for our patients and ourselves (Black 2002). An open, clinically curious, compassionate stance with ourselves increases the likelihood of owning and reclaiming our own dissociated self-states and feelings.

There was some comfort in acknowledging that I did not know my patient and that I inhabited her nonverbal affective experience, but it was not enough. On some level I knew our interactions and destabilizing affect were opening up unconscious points of connection for both of us (Black 2002). For protracted periods of time I was aroused, fantasizing not about my patient but my own sexual relational history and reliving pleasurable moments with heightened intensity. I was holding her affect and locating it in my personal sexual history. When not aroused, I felt anxious, irritable, controlled by her words and feelings. The content of the sessions seemed much less compelling than the subtext and nonverbal exchange. I struggled to make meaning.

Part of my distress was that the boundary between my self-state and my patient's self-state became blurred. Much of the experience felt like not me or alternatively too much me. It became difficult to differentiate between her projective process and my points of identification. I tried to comfort myself with theoretical understandings and was drawn to Davies and Frawley's (1994) thoughts on coercive projective identification. Did the strength and degree of my feeling dominated by this emotional state correlate with her experience of being the recipient of another's coercive projection as a child? The degree to which we bind others to our projection is a measure of the malevolence of the toxic projective-introjective process one has previously experienced (Benjamin 2002). I suspected that she had experienced such a process as a child.

My internal experience was more than I could bear alone at moments. I kept my balance by reciting theory that supported and contained me and by sharing my internal experience with trusted colleagues. Gradually, my comfort and capacity to stay with the erotic feelings and fantasies grew. I accepted that my patient needed me to join her in what felt like a dangerous process and hold the experience for both of us. She was creating "a model scene" with me of her internal relational experience. I was struggling with whose view of reality should dominate (Black 2002).

As the therapeutic relationship developed, I learned my patient had been the object of her mother's contempt. She often felt hated and hatred as a child. I came to understand how frightened she was of her own rage and of her identification with the malignant aspects of her mother. Erotic feelings comforted her and provided her with an equally powerful force field to ward off her self-loathing and rage and initiate a point of connection with me. The erotic was much more tolerable for my patient than her emptiness and sadism.

It is never helpful to ignore or deny these feelings, although it is easy to understand why a therapist might protect herself in that fashion. As therapists more openly write about and speak about sexual feelings in treatment dyads, it decreases the stigma and sense of taboo around these issues. Openness around the meaning and management of these feelings in psychotherapy increases the likelihood that therapists will view sexuality as a metaphor and not be so frightened and ashamed of these particular affects.

FORMULATING NONVERBAL EXPERIENCE

Consider the use of sexual feelings in the following case. A divorced man with one preschool son comes for an initial psychotherapy consultation. As I greet my new patient in the waiting room, I feel as if he is staring at me in a manner that makes me self-conscious and anxious. While his verbal introduction is cordial and unremarkable, I am left with the feeling that he is staring at my body, undressing me with his gaze. As he proceeds to introduce himself and his difficulties, I focus on my internal sensations and fantasies in an effort to gather more data. My mind wanders to my childhood. I recall images of myself as a young adolescent and fantasize about a recurring uncomfortable moment, walking past the high-school boys leaning on the drugstore window. I remember feeling undressed and viewed as a sexual object.

While I have no way of verifying this data yet, I privately interpret this fantasy as both a potential point of identification and an indication of a nonverbal projective process between my patient and me. I wonder if my patient is frightened of me much in the way that the high school boys frightened me as a young teen. Maybe sexual feelings shift the power dynamic with us and shield this man from feeling small and exposed in my presence? Or I wonder if this man has felt like a sexual object and been used against his will for another's sexual purposes? Perhaps he feels profoundly unsafe meeting me? I store away my hypotheses hoping to collect more data as he shares his story and we build a relationship.

As the relationship develops, I am aware of his unspoken sexual feelings and accompanying terror around our relationship. However, the feelings disquiet me. It becomes hard to differentiate between my reluctance to immerse myself in these states and the possibility that I am in direct resonance with my patient's nonverbal internal experience.

As in this case, although the vehicle for the affective symbolic communication is sexuality, sexual feelings and countertransference often defend against and disguise other affects and self states that are more intolerable, such as the terror around feeling dependent, powerless, and vulnerable. With time, this patient identifies his terror of becoming dependent and worries about safety in our relationship. Whether he can trust me or whether I will use him for my own purpose are the pressing concerns. Later in the treatment, previously suppressed traumatic memories from childhood surface. I learn this man was sexually abused as a child when he was the same age as his preschool son. This treatment became eroticized as the patient's defense against the transference, the development of a therapeutic relationship, and the remembering and revealing of his incestuous relationship with his father.

Therapists believe that countertransference phenomena usually inform us about our patients or the treatment process. Havens (1986, 1989, 1993), however, speaks of the success of treatment depending on the attitude we take toward what we discover in ourselves as well as our patients. Therapists do well to maintain an open mind about where the exploration of sexual feelings will take them. In the following case, sexual fantasies in the countertransference educate the therapist about herself as well as about her patient.

POINTS OF IDENTIFICATION

A lesbian psychiatric resident relocated to a distant city for residency and found herself evaluating a young, physically attractive, bright, lesbian graduate student. The resident experienced the patient as a warm, funny woman who was in touch with much sadness and despair around a lost relationship. She admired her patient and readily identified with her sadness and pain because she too left a complicated long-term relationship behind to accept this residency. After several meetings, the resident found herself preoccupied with thoughts of this patient in both dreaming and waking states. Her private daydreams enveloped the two in a romantic, sexual relationship building a life together. While doing errands in the city near her graduate program, she was startled by her fantasy of "bumping into" her patient. She recognized she was roaming around the city square hoping to see her. She wondered how to understand her strong feelings and fantasies about this patient and sought consultation with me.

Through the consultation and self-reflection, the resident came to view her sexual feelings and fantasies as primarily a reflection of her identification with this patient around feelings of loss and loneliness. The intensity of her affective response signaled to her the depth of her own sense of dislocation, social hunger, and isolation. Lonely, alone, working long hours in a strange city, it was easy to understand that a warm, lonely, appreciative patient might become the object of her sexual fantasies. Through her sexualized feelings for this patient, the resident became in touch with her long-standing wish to have a lover and partner that was highly educated and accomplished. Her most intimate relationships to date were with partners whom she assessed not to be intellectual or professional peers. Her patient represented her idealized love relationship.

As she became more compassionate and in touch with her own personal vulnerabilities, needs, and longings, the resident observed clearly the ways in which her patient was flirtatious and beckoned her closer. The similarities between the resident and her patient, shared life goals, and longings led the therapist to focus on the perceived similarities and not their differences. The resulting romantic feelings gratified shared needs. In this case, the synergistic effect between the therapist's vulnerabilities and unacknowledged affects and the patient's understated erotic transference resulted in an intense sexualized state for the therapist.

A RELATIONAL CONTEXT FOR UNDERSTANDING EROTIC FEELINGS AND ATTRACTION

Erotic feelings and attraction often move the treatment to an intimate affective and relational edge that may be enormously valuable and yet is difficult for both the therapist and the patient to hold and decode. The process of holding, naming, and mutually discovering the multiple relational, affective, and developmental meanings of these feelings in each treatment dyad deepens the therapeutic relationship and conversation. Therapists need to attain comfort with the feelings of attraction and sexual longings they experience with and from patients. Therapeutic inquiry is focused toward understanding the relational, transferential, countertransferential, and defensive function of such feeling states in each therapeutic dyad.

Viewing sexuality as a vehicle for intrapsychic and relational communication allows the therapist to track closely the layers of varied meaning. In the following case, the complex and shifting meaning of sexual and loving feelings between therapist and patient are illustrated with process material. My willingness to remain fluid and open to influence allows for the elaboration and unpacking of the dense and complex multiplicity of self-other configurations and meaning that my patient and I examine. While sexual and loving feelings may be profoundly unsettling for therapists as well as patients, they may also be accompanied by a sense of intimacy and closeness that is very pleasurable. Clarity concerning intrapsychic and interpersonal boundaries in the therapeutic relationship allows me to create an emotional, relational play space viewing sexuality as a metaphor. With comfort and a creative mindset, a relational approach may include spontaneity, playfulness, and humor around sexuality and loving feelings.

Education and technical assistance around these feelings in a therapeutic relationship most often happens behind closed doors in consultation, if at all. Even today, there is still very little in print that describes explicitly the tone and language of such moments in psychotherapy. There are many aspects to the unfolding of the therapeutic relationship and process with a patient. In discussing the following case, I extract and illuminate only the sexual aspect of the therapeutic relationship and conversation, focusing on my patient's expression of sexual and loving feelings and on our efforts to formulate meaning. I share our language in sessions and describe the process of decoding the self and relational metaphor.

A man shopping for a therapist arrives for an initial consultation and instantly develops a strong feeling about me. As we conclude our third meeting, he reports shyly, "I would like to work with you but there is a problem. I am attracted to you." I inquire, "The problem is?" He responds, "Isn't that against the rules? I thought if you were attracted to your therapist you couldn't be in treatment with that person." I respond, "No, it's not against the rules to have that feeling. It is a feeling like any other feeling, and it will be our job to understand what draws you close to me as well as what disappoints you, stimulates anger, or any other feeling. Social and romantic relationships with patients are against the rules, not the experience of attraction or sexual feelings. We'll study your feelings and our relationship. That's our job." Appearing pleased and excited, my patient responds, "That's great!" I respond, "You know, it's likely these feelings will shift." His affective tone deflates as he says, "I thought of that."

I am struck by my patient's openness and courage and wonder how to understand his strong feelings about me. Do I remind him of someone? How are these feelings emblematic of the developmental and relational work to be done? Is he deeply conflicted about loving and being loved? Do these feelings of attraction protect him from other feelings and vulnerabilities? Is the attraction a pleasurable distraction? Is he simply drawn to my interpersonal style or appearance?

As I begin to get to know my patient, I am charmed by his keen and quick mind, his sense of humor, fast-paced repartee, and openness. Our conversations focus on his love of women and important loving relationships in his life. While he is in fact quite depressed and despairing about himself and his life at this juncture, I come to realize that he distracts himself with thoughts of erotic feelings and me. Although at times ashamed about his feelings and thoughts, he is curious and engages with me around studying these feelings. When he asks me why I think he has such intense feelings for me, I comment, "I believe you want to begin our relationship on a high note, put your best foot forward. You want me to know about the parts of your life and your self that you feel good about and that you love. It's important to you that I understand and see your many strengths and capacities before you introduce the parts of your self that are unfinished." Erotic feelings give him a self-enhancing vehicle for saying hello to me and to test out whether I seem competent and trustworthy.

Across time, I learn about my patient's many talents and accomplishments, as well as his depression and conflicts about himself. While he has successfully formed deep and lasting relationships in his life, now he finds himself in an interpersonal drought and struggles with intense longings, self-doubts, and a harsh self-critic. He shares with me his deep worries and conflicts. Increasingly he feels safe with me, as he enjoys our sessions and finds our conversations helpful. He lets me know how much I mean to him and details his feelings of attraction and love.

The outpouring of his sexual attraction and desire shaped the early phase of engagement. The forbidden and yet compelling nature of the nonverbal affective experience fueled an especially intense experience. Playful and seductive in sessions, he muses with himself and me about the rhyme and reason for his strong attraction to me. Our initial understanding of his feelings focuses on his longings for connection and the absence of such in his life. I comment, "The intensity of your feelings for me are a signal that you would love to have a woman like me in your life. I represent the kind of person and the kind of relationship you long for but feel unable to have in the world just now." He readily accepts this but it is little comfort. While the asymmetry of our relationship provides a certain safety, it also frustrates him. As his attachment to me deepens, feelings of humiliation are stimulated. He fears the depth of his longing and of sinking into me. Criticizing himself for allowing me to become so important to him and trying to manage his intense feelings, he moves away from our relationship.

As he struggles with self-criticism and allowing himself to be deeply known and cared for, I offer the following interpretation: "You are very conflicted about your love for me, and you worry about sinking into me. On the one hand, you feel you have a safe harbor with me and you need mooring. On the other hand, you're terrified of it. You remove yourself to regulate your feelings and fantasies. We have a real relationship, of a certain sort. Yet you focus on what our relationship isn't, not on what it is. You have a good relationship with me, a close, connected, beginning therapy relationship. It speaks to your capacity to form deep close relationships with women. Yet you are taking something that is positive and turning it into something negative. You can't seem to hold on to what's good about our relationship. That's a mystery. We need to understand that."

My comments comfort my patient and soften his self-criticism, allowing him to settle into our connection. We continue to explore his feelings about himself, our relationship, and his life dilemmas. In the following session, he comments, "After the last session, I was in a great mood for days. It really helped. I feel so good about creating a good relationship with you. I want to find a way back to developing good relationships with myself and others."

He allows himself to steep in the feelings of warmth, connection, and care in our relationship, telling me, "You're a great deal." I respond, "How much you appreciate me." He continues, "Yes, and I love the way you talk to me, like last session when we were talking about my fantasies of you, and I grimaced, and you said, 'By the look on your face, I guess you know more about these fantasies than I do.' That was a really charming way to say 'Do you want to talk about your fantasies?' My fantasies are troubling. I wish I could be more open. But in order to successfully fantasize about something, I have to imagine it will or could really happen." I comment, "Are you worried about sexual behavior between us?" "Not really. I've read through the literature. I know it could never happen, that it would be detrimental to your career, and it would ruin my life," he adds with a "so they say" tone of voice. He smiles, "Maybe it would ruin my life, maybe *not*." I match his affective tone and comment: "You want me to know that part of you is willing to take that risk." He smiles. I smile and offer, "Good thing I'm the one in charge of boundaries here."

I ask, "What keeps you from using me as a symbol in your fantasies?" "I try to, but it's hard, and I hesitate to talk about it. I don't want to displease you." "Why do you worry about my displeasure? What if I was uncomfortable for a moment? What would that mean to you?" He comments, "I don't want to make you unhappy." I offer, "You worry about whether you are lovable, and my displeasure would confirm your worst feelings about yourself." We agree that he longs for my approval to soften and silence his self-doubts and self-criticism.

As the conversation shifts to my patient's anxiety around his financial situation and compulsion about paying me on time, I wonder aloud what his worry is about paying on time. He smiles with a twinkle in his eye and comments, "I have an idea. How about this? I could suspend paying you.

We could see what feelings and fantasies come up for me. You and I would discuss them. Let's experiment with this for six months." Again, I match his tone and offer, "You took your compulsion about paying me on time and turned it on its ear." I playfully comment, "You're flirting with me!" He responds, "Is that flirting, to tease about money?" "No," I say, "It's a verbal fantasy of moving our relationship out of the professional realm." "Yes, I guess it is."

My upcoming vacation stimulates anxiety in my patient. He plans a trip, leaving before I depart and returning after I return. Our vacations provide an opportunity to focus on the meaning and value of our relationship and identify what he will miss about me and our time. He is able to identify many features, but focuses on the pleasure and comfort of my company and our conversations. He loves the way I speak to him and details the specifics of our conversational dance that he finds so helpful and pleasing. He will miss me and worries how he will keep himself company in my absence. We wonder if he will be harsh with himself in my absence.

After our last session, we speak on the phone briefly. He calls back immediately and leaves a message. He worries that he has offended me unknowingly in some manner, as evidenced by his perception of an abrupt ending to our phone conversation. I return his call and comment with energy, "Don't torture yourself; don't go there. I will miss you, and I will think of you. Have a great trip. I'll see you when I return." When he returns from vacation, he tells me how much that comment helped him shift his self-state and his internal climate back to a warm feeling of connection accompanied by the sense that he was okay.

Over time, my patient's worries and conflicts about himself and forming a love relationship outside the consulting room focus our work. He remains both compelled by his feelings for me and intolerant. He is enraged at himself for the depth of his feelings and attachment; I offer the following frame: "It makes perfect sense to me that you would love me. I am devoted to you. I don't ask you for anything, except money, and that does not matter much to you. And there is enough distance in our relationship so that you feel safe. I think it's easy to understand why you would love me." This explanation makes sense to my patient and helps him to soften his self-punishing stance.

We focus our work to understand the nuances of our connection and his fantasies. He concludes that he is in fact attracted to me for the reasons discussed. While I believe that to be true and tell him so, I again encourage him to view these feelings as a mental mechanism with dynamic relational meaning as well. He responds by restating that he really finds me attractive. I respond, "Yes, I know you are attracted to me. There are qualities about me that you find appealing and draw you close to me. And you use these feelings for psychological purposes. Your attraction also shields you from other feelings like feeling small and vulnerable. Like in this session when you were expressing your fears and doubts about yourself, your internal climate and the emotional climate between us shifted to your erotic feelings about me. You are very conflicted about allowing yourself to be nurtured, and you use erotic feelings to distract yourself from your need for nurturance. You don't have to choose between whether your attraction is real or serves psychological purposes. Both are true. I'm suggesting we understand these feelings of attraction in a complex manner, studying the layers of meaning."

As my patient dips deeper into the depth of his despair and self-worry, the intensity of the erotic and loving feelings deepens as well, providing a much-needed and welcome relief from his anguish. He fantasizes about his feelings, our relationship, and me. He tells me how much he likes me and wishes I were in his life. I grow to understand how much company I provide for him both in sessions and during the week. "Not having other relationships with women now must intensify your longings and feelings with me. I imagine it's difficult. Part of what makes me so important to you is that you have lost faith in your capacity to attract a woman like me in your life. You must worry you will be stuck here endlessly." He confirms these fears. I offer comfort and reassurance by commenting, "I do not share these worries. I see and feel differently about you and these matters. I can feel close and connected to you, and that would not be possible without your full participation. I believe you will make a loving relationship in the world again, maybe not as soon as you would like. I know how worried you are, but your strong attachment to the idea that nobody that you would want would want you is of interest. Let's try to understand that myth."

Tormented by desire and arousal in my presence, my patient remains intermittently despairing about his capacity to create such a connection in the world. He is genuinely confused about which feelings arise from him, including which capacities he might possess. In a session, he expresses a desire to show me an erotic picture of his body, adding that he would not, however, do anything like that. I respond, "Let's talk about it. What would you like me to know when I view your photo? What are you hoping I might feel?" He responds, "I want you to see my body. See that I'm an attractive, potent man. I feel so small with you, like a child." I respond, "I believe you want to be sure that I know you are a vital, sexually competent man and that your sexual self is a very important and pleasurable part of you." He agrees. I continue, "I do wonder if by showing me this photo you will be turning the tables between us around feelings of desire. You have felt so tormented by your arousal and desire with me; perhaps you want me to see what I'm missing and to be filled with desire for you. You would much prefer to be the object of my desire and arousal than to hold those feelings for me." He smiles and comments, "I would like to be the object of your desire. It would make me feel so much better about myself."

As he experiments with becoming more engaged in the world of relationships, sexual feelings, desire, and closeness in our relationship shift back and forth between background and foreground. He feels deeply known, accepted, and loved in our relationship, which is a source of comfort and provides him with an inner sense of well-being and company. Keeping my presence internally and feeling loved shift his sense of himself and facilitate his engagement with others in myriad ways.

After a disappointing effort to forge a new connection, he is filled with despair and anger and returns to his desire for me as a retreat from the relational world and feeling disappointed. He continues with his despair by saying, "I just don't like anyone as much as I like you." I respond, "A large part of my appeal is the structure of our relationship, and the fact you can't have me." He knows. Tormented by his feelings of desire, he wonders is this good for him? I comment, "Our relationship and work is in part a study in disappointment. Bearing the feelings of closeness and disappointment has made you stronger and better able to bear disappointments within yourself and in life." He agrees but he does not like it.

After a series of painful disappointments, he shares with me "his irrational feelings" that "if you really cared for me, you would have an extra-therapeutic relationship with me." I offer him the following frame: "You long to be special. Having an extra-therapeutic relationship with me would be special. You are so drawn to feeling special that you are willing to hold out for me or have nothing. You know you can't have me in that way, and yet you are willing to have nothing. It's hard for you to accept that you can't have what you want and move on. Your erotic attachment to me keeps you from confronting disappointment. It's a very self-punishing stance."

Determined to master his anxiety and relational learning edge, with me firmly planted internally, my patient deepens and varies his engagement with women and the relational world. Experimenting with relationships, he declares his wish to practice getting into and out of close relationships with women and to give himself the space and freedom to practice his new relational and affective capacities. As he increases his engagement with others, he continues to study his connection to me and brings in outside connections to process.

DISCUSSION OF CASE

As is evident in this case, sexual and loving feelings are both real and embody a multiplicity of self-other configurations and wide-ranging affect. Open and available for my patient's varied use of me and our relationship, I follow his lead and use the role and affective experience that I find myself in. He is re-creating a story line depicting powerful organizing experiences and feelings from his childhood. Re-creating multiple, complex affective and relational scenarios from his past with me, sexual feelings are vehicles of communication and a metaphor about self and other. We identify and hold the layers of shifting intrapsychic and relational meaning while honoring the depth of our connection and the feelings between us. Sexual and loving feelings allow this man to enter into a deep personal engagement with himself and me. Wishing to be acknowledged as a passionate sexual being, he longs to consolidate these feelings about himself. The enduring question is: Would a woman he wants want him?

Sexuality is a powerful communication about his feeling state. It also distracts and protects him from other intolerable feelings such as despair, anger, loneliness, and disappointment. He longs to be nurtured and admired in a sustaining self-other relationship that is expressed in sexual terms in the transference. In part this is because he so wishes to be an object of desire, and in part it is to protect him from his feeling small, unlovable, and angry. Part of him would like to be very special to me, as he lacks faith in his capacity to develop such an intimate connection in the world and because sinking into me allows him to avoid the anxiety around his developmental and relational learning edge.

Loving me so allows him to delay finding a love relationship in the world and confronting the anxiety and self-issues such a connection would stir. At times, I felt he was employing his desire for me as a retreat from the relational world and as a way to manage his anxiety about transitions and disappointments. His idealized love for me has both regressive and progressive elements; it relives old scenarios and opens up and unpacks new terrain. It is self-enhancing and limiting, pleasurable and self-punishing, a new affective and relational experience and an all too familiar reenactment.

While we both acknowledged the depth of our connection and examined his erotic and loving feelings, much of what was communicated and that transpired between us was nonverbal. Feeling the depth of our mutual connection and the unspoken but deeply felt range of our shared experience was very valuable to this man. The warmth, playfulness, and moments of lightness, tension, and pleasure only added to the depth of our connection and paved the way for deep examination of the multiple elaborations of his self-other conflicts and feelings. He needed to capture my full and deep attention and be emotionally held close while shifting through a range of self-other feeling states and enactments. The feelings cocreated in our relationship allowed me to become a positive, enduring intrapsychic presence that gave him a buoyancy and aliveness with himself and others. It was more possible than ever for my patient to be both an observer of and immersed in this affective and relational process. With his emerging relational knowledge in hand, he engaged in new ways with others.

HOLDING AND FORMULATING AGGRESSIVE FEELINGS

Therapists are nearly as conflicted about aggression in therapeutic relationships as they are about sexuality. As therapists, we often come to this work with a deep personal investment in the role of healer. Hoffman (2002) facetiously comments that we have "chosen this line of work for past crimes and failures." Davies (2002) speaks of a therapist's "preferred version of self" that is devoid of negative toxic states and bad internal objects, preferring to assign those states to our patients. Maroda (1991) speaks about the therapist's wish to be healed and to heal our loved ones through the transformational process of psychotherapy. If out of touch with our wishes of "reclaiming ourselves through reclaiming our patients," therapists may fashion a practice style that colludes with our patients' grandiose fantasies of being healed and avoids deep engagement around painful growth-producing conversations and enactments (Maroda 1991, p. 23).

Evil, badness, malignant feelings, and toxic states of contempt and self-loathing may be as difficult for us to bear as for our patients (Winnicott 1958). Yet we know and understand that, as therapists, if we are to facilitate transforming growth and developmental change, we must be open and willing to relive the dark and most damaging affective and relational scenarios with our patients. Paul Russell, in describing "the crunch," his term for the inevitable and invaluable transference/countertransference enactments that carry the seeds of developmental possibilities, outlines how the patient needs the "analyst to occupy two mutually exclusive places at the same time" (Mitchell 1988, p. 53). The patient needs the analyst to be fully drawn into the repetition, taking on an assigned affective and relational role and to be a new and different affective relationship in the here and now. Reliving and negotiating through this paradox is essential to growth and the very essence of psychotherapy (S. A. Pizer 1992, 1996; Russell 1976a, 1976b, 1976c). Out of re-creating the old, new growth and development become possible.

Russell liked to comment that the only real resistance in psychotherapy is the therapist's resistance to feeling fully the patient's feelings and experience (1983). To overcome our resistance to feeling the patient's feelings and be open to occupying the countertransference requires discipline and conscious effort. In this process, the therapist's own internalized bad objects and negative affects inevitably become mobilized and infuse the relational matrix. As Davies (2002) suggests in her lecture "Whose Bad Objects Are These Anyway?", the emergence of internalized bad objects commonly stimulates the therapist's shame and guilt. Under these conditions, there will likely be a mutual reciprocal projective process wherein the therapist dissociates and assigns her toxic affects and identifications to her patient just as her patient does to her.

Ogden's (1994) "subjugating analytic third" describes this process of cross-identification, wherein the therapist's and patient's preexisting identifications become mobilized and mutually engaged in the repetition. Benjamin (1998) fully elaborates this projective dance, describing the "structure of complementarity wherein the therapist continually reverses positions with her patient through identifications creating a web of entanglements and polarities" (p. xiv). The way out of the web of identifications and reversal of positions is for the therapist to create *the third*, "an internal mental space for true observation that arises out of dialogue" and mutual recognition (Benjamin 1998, p. xv). The third is a mental spiritual space that allows for multiple realities to coexist and be deeply understood in the therapeutic relationship. This space allows the therapist to be an observer and a participant in the reoccurring web of identifications and reversals of position.

As a young therapist, I found it intolerable to hate my patients and was only slightly more comfortable with my patients hating me. While I understood the necessity of my patient struggling with her toxic states and identifications, it was much less clear to me that I, too, would become deeply engaged in an internal parallel process. Rage and hatred in therapeutic relationships startled and frightened me. Later I realized how worried I was of my own negative affects and identifications.

Early in my career, I treated a woman who had been the object of her mother's contempt and hatred and who developed similar feelings for me. I found the intensity of her hatred destabilizing and felt simply overwhelmed and confused sitting with her. I imagine this was an element of her experience as well. Consciously struggling to regain my equilibrium, I presented this case frequently to Paul Russell, relying on his words to comfort and contain my patient and me. Before each session with this patient, I read and reread Paul's supervisory comments, hoping to evoke his spirit and wisdom. I hoped his presence would give me the courage to simply remain emotionally open and present with my patient. It was difficult, even impossible at times. Convinced of my uselessness as a therapist to this woman, I was stunned when she informed me that she was applying to graduate school and wished to become a therapist like me. My willingness to struggle with my process and to be as emotionally vulnerable as I could bear in the service of developing a new healing relationship had been of value to her, although I could not see it at the time.

VARIED MEANINGS OF HATRED AND RAGE

Patients' experience of aggressive feelings toward therapists represent and communicate a wide range of affective experiences, self and developmental difficulties, and interpersonal conflicts and needs. While inherently threatening and potentially destabilizing, hatred and rage have considerable dynamic and relational value (Epstein 1977; Gabbard 1996; Gabbard and Lester 1995; Kernberg 1992). Rage and hate may be a symbolic marker, distraction, or disguise for numerous other affects and phenomena. Some of the more common are to organize the amorphous self; a reenactment of traumatic relational scenarios; and as a defense against more positive affects or to defend against self-injury, dependency, grief, and powerlessness. In general, aggression serves to rid the self of intense intolerable internal affects or self-objects.

Hatred may ward off psychosis or feelings of disintegration and may function to restore a sense of internal equilibrium. Or, hatred may disguise and distract against longings for love, nurturance, grief, and envy, or serve to regulate interpersonal distance and self-boundaries.

For patients who have experienced a malignant projective process as children and a profoundly neglectful or hostile interpersonal environment, positive feelings and relationships stimulate conflict and terror. The development of positive states may be accompanied by an exacerbation of self-attack through unconscious identifications (Epstein 1977; Frankel 2000; Gabbard 1996; Robbins 2000). These patients may need malignant internal objects for a sense of self-cohesion. They feel lost without hatred that structures and organizes the internal experience. Traumatized patients may experience rage and hatred as they attempt to master the early rage and destructiveness of traumatic experience.

Hatred may signal a wish for revenge or loyalty to one's family of origin. It also may provide both a sense of continuity for the patient and a point of attachment. A patient may sustain a connection through negative affect because positive attention is unfamiliar and disorganizing.

Hatred and masochism commonly coexist. Revenge against the self is common and may be a constant companion serving myriad purposes. Revenge fantasies represent traumatic reenactment, defensive shields, and more adaptive progressive strivings. Horowitz (2004) suggests that masochism functions to restore the early dyad experience and may be a remedy for loneliness. Both torturer and victim reside internally and provide a certain sort of company. Masochist fantasies provide an antidote to intolerable loneliness.

FORMULATING EXPERIENCE

For sexually or physically traumatized patients, sexual and aggressive feelings are confused and confusing to patients and sometimes therapists. Often, with traumatized patients, sexually explicit and aggressive material defends against the terror associated with object relations. The patient's sexualized aggressive material sometimes alienates and frightens the therapist. When a person has been abused and violated by caretakers under the guise of parenting, all relationships become infused with distorted sexual and aggressive elements that are ego-syntonic. Such use of sexual material and behavior diagnoses the patient's difficulties and etches out the therapeutic work to be done. Inevitably and predictably, such dynamics manifest themselves in the treatment relationship, presenting the therapist often with offensive and sadistic sexual material to understand and manage. Patients with trauma histories are prone to ego-syntonic, eroticized transferences that are intense, repetitive, and all consuming (Gabbard 1993).

> A married man with a history of severe sexual and physical abuse during childhood presented for treatment of his depression and anger. After several sessions, the patient informed his female therapist about his visits to prostitutes immediately following therapy appointments. He continued, "I call her by your name. I pretend she is you." The therapist, frightened, disgusted, and overwhelmed by this sexually sadistic material, sat quietly,

privately wishing to terminate the session and her patient on the spot. The next session her patient returned and announced, "I have an erection. Maybe I should walk around the block to cool off." Feeling assaulted and enraged, the therapist sought a consultation to manage her feelings and sort out the best therapeutic strategy for this patient.

The therapist wondered why she felt so powerless and assaulted by her patient's aggression and his erection. She became aware that her patient's behavior reminded her of her father, a harsh, controlling man. Despite the therapist's best efforts to please her father or protect herself from his stinging comments, she felt devastated by his criticism of her. Feeling inadequate, powerless, and unable to stand up to her father, the therapist developed a compensatory strategy of splitting off her anger and disappointment and being only helpful. These dynamics and feelings, rooted in the therapist's early familial relationships, helped explain her horror and contempt for her patient.

While her patient was ostensibly discussing sexual feelings and material, the interpersonal communication was really about aggression, interpersonal safety, and respect. It also represented the terror associated with being in another's presence. The therapist's unresolved anger toward her father and difficulty tolerating rage in the transference contributed to her countertransferential difficulties.

When sexual feelings represent feelings of terror and sadism, therapeutic limit setting may be necessary to protect participants and the treatment process. Therapists' inability to deal with their own and their patient's sexualized aggression often leads to countertransference withdrawal and treatment failures. Subtly, therapists communicate to patients that such material and difficulties are so abhorrent that no one can tolerate it, and patients leave treatment.

With the benefit of consultation, the therapist recognized her patient's offensive and sadistic presentation as representing a defense against his terror of being violated again by a person in power. To protect himself from feelings of vulnerability and powerlessness, he became the potent perpetrator aggressing against her. The therapist recalled that many of his significant childhood object relations included sexual exploitation. He was reenacting these scenarios with her as the victim.

Applying her relational understanding of his sexual talk and her issues, the therapist compassionately shared her concerns about creating a safe treatment milieu for both participants. The therapist responded, "In your talk about prostitutes I hear wishes and concerns for our relationship. Because of your history, it's understandable that you believe all relationships involve a sexual component. Perhaps it's hard to know just how to be with another person without someone being used, without consent, in a sexual way. Our relationship and your treatment will not include sexual behavior. We need to create a safe space for you to get the help you deserve with your depression and anger. Psychotherapy is a verbal treatment. There will be no physical contact."

As therapists, we are much more comfortable analyzing and studying our patients' affective and relational dilemmas and much less comfortable examining our personal contribution to the web of identifications. Predictably, our patients' anger or devaluation stimulates the reemergence of our personally distressing negative affects. Identifications that may be out of our awareness and difficult to possess become activated. An honest, open, self-reflective stance is most valuable to the patient and to the relational process. It may ultimately increase the therapist's self-knowledge.

A woman with a history of a painful childhood comes for treatment. Several previous courses of psychotherapy with senior clinicians were unsatisfying and unhelpful. One therapist was kindly, but not deep enough or smart enough. The other therapist's stance continually injured and insulted her, stimulating her feeling misunderstood and enraged. In each case she stayed long enough to do some personal work but eventually left feeling dissatisfied. I begin the relationship with her on a tentative note in part because of her high expectations for me and in part because of her series of disappointments with others. I counsel myself to remain open to an uncharted relational and therapeutic journey. I succeed in awakening my sense of interest and curiosity in beginning treatment with a new person.

In short order, I am uncomfortable and begin to dread her sessions. Despite my best efforts to understand her experience and her feelings, she is chronically annoyed with me, which is communicated through verbal transactions and nonverbal pathways. She offers me supervisory help with what feels like a measure of contempt. I feel controlled by her and irritated. After a particularly difficult series of sessions, when I hear her voice on my answering machine, I bristle and think, "What does she want now? I don't have time to return her call. She can wait." I know as a child she felt abandoned and coerced into her father's image of her, but isn't it time she outgrew these feelings and took more responsibility for herself and her feelings?

Allowing myself to air my internal dialogue, including my negativity about this woman, captures my supervisory attention. I was struck with how punishing my internal voice was and how unyielding I felt in response to her. Drawn to formulations that locate the anger and devaluation squarely within her, I feel like an object from her past that she was punishing and denigrating. Understanding my internal distress as a function of projective identification quiets me and allows me to feel righteous momentarily. While this internal stance of moral superiority soothes me, it is of no therapeutic use with my patient. She is as convinced that I am the problem as I am certain that these negative affects arise from her.

Monitoring my internal experience, I realize I am angry with this woman. In moments, she reminds me of family members who were critical and held me responsible for their own feeling states. Recognizing my contribution to this cycle of reversal of positions helped me to realign myself with my patient. I became more compassionate with myself around the activation of my anger and internalized scenarios. As a result I experienced more compassion for my patient around her hatred and devaluation of me. I was able to be more giving with her. My self-awareness shifted my internal emotional climate and the emotional climate between us. This shift allowed me to structure a process wherein her contempt for me and my contempt was discussed more openly. Commenting that "I know how angry you must be with me because I knew how angry I feel when I sit with you," acknowledged our mutual state of hostility. My comment initiated a more direct conversation about these feelings and our relationship.

Sometimes, despite our conscious efforts, acknowledging and identifying our contribution to the web of identifications is impossibly difficult. An outside perspective from trusted peers or a consultant may facilitate this process. But it is painful, and therapists may be avoidant. A patient who struggled with envy and contempt and simultaneously wanted more from me asked a seemingly simple question about travel plans. I bristled with an intense visceral response that left me with no internal or relational room to maneuver. In some ways, it felt irrational, but my predominant experience was that these feelings emanated from her, that she was angry.

I felt as if her question was hostile or intrusive. Mired in an angry, un-yielding space, I was convinced that my response was a reaction to her unacknowledged anger and resentment. Discussing the case with col-leagues allowed me to view the abject dissonance between my internal feelings and my patient's request and prompted further self-analysis. Without the benefit of my colleagues' support and perspective, I might have remained mired in this negative self-state. Identifying the relational scenario that I was replaying with my patient allowed me to untangle the points of identification and shift to another self-state.

These cycles of mutual projective identification may be destructive in a therapeutic relationship. Yet how tenaciously we, as therapists, cling to our desired view of ourselves. The shame and guilt stirred by our nega-tive self-states and relational scenarios are hard to bear. This, of course, stimulates more reliance on a projective process as a means of reestab-lishing our internal equilibrium (Benjamin 2002; Frankel 2002; Robbins 2000). Benjamin's concept of *the third* allows us to remain present with our patients' intrapsychic and relational reality while owning our internal experience as well.

In a session, I share an observation with a patient about her anger that I imagine will be difficult for her to hear. But I believe it holds important information for her to consider. My observation stimulates shame, and she quickly becomes defensive and argumentative. I try my best to tem-per her self-judgment and externalized rage at me. I attempt to more fully explain to her my thoughts and feelings and why I think this conversation is of value. She will not hear of it, as she is convinced that I am being harshly judgmental and hurting her. I am convinced that she is being un-duly harsh with herself and me. My comments also set into motion an old, familiar relational scenario. I become her abusive mother in this transaction. Clearly she is injured and enraged and I imagine struggling to ward off her inflamed self-judgment around this issue. We end the ses-sion with her storming out of my office exuding shame and rage, slam-ming the door. I am left wondering if this was helpful.

After the session, I receive several enraged voice messages from my pa-tient lambasting me for injuring and insulting me. "I want you to know you really hurt me. Why do you speak to me in that manner? So mean-spirited and negative! I thought you are supposed to be a professional, but you seem so incompetent and inept, and it leaves me feeling that you must be trying to hurt me. Your comments demonize me and view me in a negative light. I am not a bad person. You have a very negative effect upon me, and while you have been very helpful in general, sessions like this make me think about not coming back."

My patient's message stimulates a visceral response. I stiffen as I hear her accusations: "mean-spirited, incompetent, inept, hurtful." At first, I am certain that she is externalizing her self-judgment. My comments may have been hard to hear, but certainly not mean-spirited. I feel a strong internal resistance about allowing myself to go there emotionally. I realize her comments stimulate my self-judgment. Maybe I chose the wrong time to raise this material? Perhaps I might have selected other language? Was my tone negative and harsh, as she reports? I did not feel angry with her in the session. But I was as intent in making my point as she was in deflecting my message. Internally disrupted, I wrestle with myself to regain my equilibrium. Vacillating between the belief that my patient really has a conflict with this aspect of herself and wondering if perhaps the problem was in my presentation to her, I struggle to locate a more comfortable space. I wonder how we will continue this conversation.

Internally revisiting my relationship with this woman, I reexperience the full range of my close and connected feelings. I am very fond of this woman and am sad and sorry that I was so unhelpful. As a way to comfort myself, I return to theoretical constructs that guide my work, and I hope to move myself along into a different and more relational space. Associating to family conversations that have not gone well, I realize that I have occupied this space before. The scenario involves my raising a difficult subject matter with my children. Something about my tone or the seriousness of my delivery startles and frightens the other, maybe stimulating shame. Now I shift to my patient and imagine there was something about my tone or my presentation intersecting with her harshness and anxiety about this aspect of herself.

In the next session, I comment, "May I begin?" My patient responds, "Yes." I continue, "I am sorry I hurt you. I heard your feedback, and I'm thinking about it. I believe that there is a valuable opportunity here. The reasons we occupied such a painful and unhelpful space are layered and complex. There is something for me to learn here about myself, and there is something for you to learn here about your internal experience. Then there is something to learn about the transaction between us. I take your feedback seriously, and I am studying what I did that was hurtful and what I might have done differently. I believe that there was something about my tone of voice or choice of words, something that was not helpful and even hurtful. I'm thinking about that. Anything more you can tell me about that and what it meant to you will be of help."

My patient responds, "What a relief. I'm so glad you said that. I was so worried that you would blame me for this. It means a lot to me that you take responsibility. Your tone of voice scared me, I think." I inquire, "What was it exactly?" She responds, "You sounded anxious, maybe alarmed. I thought 'Oh, my god, something is really wrong with me.' You wouldn't be that worried unless this was really bad." I continue, "My tone of voice alarmed you and shifted you into a state of self-worry." "Yes, I am very worried about treating others the way my mother treated me, being mean-spirited and, well, abusive. I felt you were saying I was my mother or like my mother." I comment, "I stimulated your worry and feeling that you are like your mother. You are very critical of the part of you that reminds you of your mother's rage. And you are worried about your anger." My patient responds, "My anger scares me, and sometimes I do feel something is wrong with me, especially when I want to hurt somebody. We do need to talk about my anger, but it's hard for me. I feel so ashamed."

Creating a relational frame that emphasizes the belief that my patient and I coconstructed this moment facilitates the repair of the injury. It also leads us back to attunement. The cross-identifications between my patient and myself led to this relational encounter. Following my openness and full acceptance of my negative contribution, my patient is able to return to her internal experience and begin to explore her deep worries around her anger. The enactment and movement to a new relational space facilitated deeper exploration around her shame and anger. Now, more than before, her conflicted identification with her mother could be explored. The transaction between us, including the process of negotiation, led my patient to expanded knowledge about how to conduct oneself in a relationship around conflict and making meaning.

As Hoffman reminds us:

> In times of stress and ambiguity, therapists struggle with the balance between conflicting motives and allegiances in assessing how to proceed. . . . In either case, the work requires an underlying tolerance for uncertainty and with it a radical, yet critical kind of openness that is conveyed over time in various ways, including a readiness to soul-search, to negotiate, and to change. The bad object that is lurking in every analytic situation is the one that pulls either of the participants into absolute commitment to one side of his or her conflict (for example, the side that wants to analyze) with the result that the other side (for example, the side that wants to respond in a more spontaneous, personal way) must be abandoned and repressed (1994, p. 215).

A patient knows and does not know the relational ways in which she is, despite her abhorrence, in fact like her sadistic father and her brother. Our work had focused upon increasing her awareness of her internal struggle with these sadomasochistic identifications. Overwhelmed and confused around these identifications, she is genuinely baffled about who did what to whom in our painful exchanges during sessions. A multitude of impasses and bouts of destabilizing enactments tested our relationship. Across time, these "crunches" served to increase our understanding of her internal relational grid and the commingling of cross-identifications. Ultimately, negotiating these conflicts resulted in a deeper connection.

After a series of rageful sessions, a comment from me stimulates toxic affects. Feelings of victimization erupt within my patient, and then between us, resulting in internal and interpersonal turbulence. Rapidly, her identification with her sadistic parent mobilizes. She speaks to me with offensive language and in a contemptuous manner, berating my comments and my person at length. Acknowledging these identifications has been a developmental process for my patient. Now, for perhaps the first time, she more fully possesses this self-state. After this provocative and contemptuous exchange, she is now humiliated as well by her cruel behavior toward me.

Her self-observing capacity kicks in, leading her to worry that she may have wrecked our good relationship. She is worried that I will not want to work with her any longer. As a result of repetition and perhaps a little luck, this exchange has not unduly stimulated my preexisting identifications. Now, after many similar go-rounds, I do not feel flooded with negative emotions, and I possess affective clarity about this exchange.

I offer the following comments: "You are very conflicted about your anger, and you worry that your anger will destroy our connection as it has ruptured other relationships for you. I see and feel even more clearly why you are worried. Your anger takes you to an altered state with yourself and in relationships. My comment hurt your feelings. It stimulated your feelings of being abused and dominated by your mother. Those feelings shifted you into your identification with your mother. It's as if I became you as a small child in that interaction. You were treating me the way you treat yourself internally. Now I have a very clear feeling about how mean you can be to yourself."

She comments, "I worry you won't want to work with me. I feel you don't like me anymore." I respond, "You don't like yourself when you are in that self-state. That's why it's so hard for you to face this part of yourself. You hate it." "Yes, it's true. I don't know what to do with these feelings. I know that I am mean, and I say hurtful things." Now, weeping, she comments, "I am sorry I was mean to you."

I offer, "I am very fond of you. I feel I know you well, including your many strengths. I have a great deal of compassion for you and your developmental journey. At times, you behave in a manner that makes it difficult for me to feel kindly toward you. Your behavior provokes anger and leads others to lash out at you, to mistreat you. We need to understand what might be your motive in behaving toward others in a manner that provokes mistreatment? It's not comfortable, but it's a good sign that your anger is so present in our relationship. Our work may increase your compassion and understanding of these aspects of yourself."

Naming the repetition without trying to control my patient or shift the relational paradigm creates space for novel intersubjective encounters. This encounter also leads to shifts in my patient's sense of self and of me. Re-creating and surviving the repetitive replaying in the transference/

countertransference of this familiar scenario offers a reparative developmental opportunity. In slowly elaborating my patient's emotional state and conflicted identifications, our interactions differentiate our relationship from her internal object world.

Ringstrom (2004) suggests enactments function, in part, as homeostatic regulators. In this case, the repetitive replaying of this toxic scenario served to regulate emotional states and the threat of change. The enactment regulates interpersonal distance and is a shield against frightening shifts away from the familiar. Through the renegotiation of the repetition, my patient enters into an in-between state, no longer dominated by the repetition. It is a state of heightened vulnerability and openness. My patient's capacity to be introspective, fluid, and open to influence increases.

With redundancy and repetition, gradually her sense of self and other expands, increasing emotional complexity and coherence. Her emotional states become more modulated. The repetitive re-creating and then deconstructing of old relational scenarios leads to a crisis of attachment (B. Pizer 2003; S. A. Pizer 1992; Stern 2002). It also destabilizes existing structures, followed by a deeper engagement and a more complex and inclusive understanding of self and other.

Some of the aforementioned enactments pulled me out of connection with my patients. I withdrew into my internal experience and moved away from a dyadic negotiating stance. At these moments, it is challenging to remember emotionally that we do not have to collapse the possibility of ways to understand this moment into either/or. When confronted with these ubiquitous and inevitable enactments with our patients, we will be better able to hold a relational perspective if we can strengthen our capacity to withstand the activation of our identifications. Taking full responsibility for our contribution allows us to realign ourselves with our patient and study the complexity of meaning. Such realignment opens up negotiating space to facilitate the emergence of other self-states, bridging relational realities and returning to attunement with our patients. The negotiation of these small impasses requires that therapists yield to a negotiating stance and coconstruct with their patient the transition into another self and affective state.

Open internal boundaries allow therapists to receive patients' unconscious communications and to hold disavowed affects and self-states that
make possible new relational and affective development. Projective identification and enactment provide the conceptual frames for unpacking the
layers of affective communication between therapist and patient, and they
provide a cognitive structure for keeping one's balance at vexing moments. Such deep engagement with patients inevitably stirs intense feelings that may be difficult for therapists to bear. Unwanted affect and unconscious points of identification with patients may stimulate therapists'
shame and guilt, leading to states of disequilibrium. A therapeutic stance
that is fluid and open to intrapsychic and interpersonal influence allows
for the experience and elaboration of complex unconscious affects,
points of identification, and self-other configurations. Clarity concerning
intrapsychic and interpersonal boundaries in the therapeutic relationship
is most helpful.

4

EXCEPTIONAL
REQUESTS IN
THE THERAPEUTIC
RELATIONSHIP

Patients regularly deliver into the psychotherapeutic relationship their most painful and shameful feelings about themselves and their relationships through special requests. Such requests often require a stretching of the usual treatment frame or call for an authentic personal response from the therapist. The understanding and negotiation of the request involves deep personal engagement of both participants. It represents heightened opportunities for significant shifts in affective experience and relational knowledge. At these moments our patients are engaged in a relational transaction that provides a unique window into their inner experience. The patient's experience of recognition, that is "knowing that one is known" is central to this endeavor (Sander 2002). A critical moment opens up for the possibility of expanding specificity of recognition that shifts the patient's sense of self-as-agent. (Lyons-Ruth 1999, 2000; Sander 2002; Stern et al. 1998). These requests often represent extraordinary events or require interventions that are not routinized in everyday practice, although they do not violate ethical codes.

Therapists who subscribe to an intersubjective relational approach favor a process of mutual discovery between therapist and patient. This process relies upon *implicit relational knowing* to lay the foundation for the development of *shared relational knowledge* between them. With far greater freedom to decide what is therapeutic, relational therapists face many more choices when confronted with exceptional requests or unexpected moments. By emphasizing the transforming power of new relational experiences with a therapist, often the therapeutic work is up close and personal in the transference/countertransference and in the interpersonal therapeutic relationship. Therapists' willingness to explore and keep open the possibility of unusual interventions in the service of expanding new experience of self and other is most valuable, although it may be uncomfortable.

MOTHER-INFANT STUDIES AND MUTATIVE ACTION IN THERAPY

Infant studies inform us that both infant and caretaker express affect and comprehend the affective expression of the other through nonverbal systems (Lyons-Ruth 1999, 2000, 2003; Sanders 2002; Stern et al. 1998; Tronick et al. 1998). The importance of social connectedness and mutual regulation of affect in a bidirectional relational matrix can give rise to new affective and self-organization. Procedural knowledge advances for both participants. Therapists' comfort and capacity to hold and use these personal sensings of self and patient to reorganize and expand states of consciousness and ways of being are developmentally valuable.

Sander's (2002) notion of "moments of meeting," an event that "rearranges implicit relational knowing for patient and therapist alike" (Stern et al. 1998, p. 906), becomes a shaping theoretical construct as one approaches the subject of unusual requests. In the therapeutic relationship, shared relational knowing comprises intersubjective moments between patient and therapist that open up the possibility of new organization both within and between the participants (Stern et al. 1998). Most importantly, these moments produce structural shifts and alter the patient's *ways of being* (Stern et al. 1998, p. 905).

Relational therapists recognize that moments of therapeutic change most often occur outside the routine discourse of the therapeutic relationship. Jean Baker Miller (2000) identifies how developmentally valuable therapeutic exchanges most often occur outside the therapist's "comfort zone" and may represent novel interventions.

Moments of meeting call into question the familiar, safe, intersubjective environment between therapist and patient. The intersubjective relationship may be disrupted or ruptured depending on how the therapist responds (Stern et al. 1998). These moments require that the therapist respond in a novel, personal, and authentic manner that is crafted to fit this moment and this relationship with this patient. An emotionally honest, revealing response will increase the patient's implicit relational knowing of self and therapist and their relationship (Stern et al. 1999). Handcrafted to fit the specificity of this moment within this therapeutic dyad, the therapist's response is unique. It is a moment filled with great therapeutic potential and great risk. At these times, a therapist may experience undue anxiety and uncertainty because they sense the great potential and great risk.

While openness to moments of meeting and unusual interventions carry the possibility of enhancing relatedness between therapist and patient, it also leaves therapists without a technical compass for negotiating through high-risk, high-gain therapeutic moments. Therapists who rely upon their internal sensations to guide relational formulations and interventions may find comfort in a theory and an approach that lends itself to such. Other therapists may feel unnerved and unsettled by the absence of defining parameters and specific technical guidelines for interventions with patients. Therapists' probing self-scrutiny is required to fully understand their own interest and influence on the clinical process (Ehrenberg 1992; Gabbard 1995; Gabbard and Lester 1995; Maroda 1991, 1999a, 1999b, 2000; McLaughlin 1991, 1995, 1996, 2000).

GUIDING PARAMETERS

My personal practice policies include no post-termination relationships, no therapeutic secrets, and honoring the code of ethics and the fiduciary relationship. All other therapeutic choices are negotiable. On occasion I employ physical touch and out-of-office contact, accept gifts, and give gifts. Furthermore, I seriously consider all other unusual requests. My decision around therapeutic interventions depends on the particulars of the individual case and the mutually coconstructed meaning of what is being negotiated. As best as I can, I assess what intervention or conversation will move us along toward expanded relational knowing and new forms of relational organization. These treatment boundaries leave the space and the freedom to tailor my responses and interventions to recognize the unique aspects of interpersonal and intrapsychic moments. Case by case, I tailor my response to the specifics at hand, not bound by technique or theory. As I confront a moment or a request, I am thinking what will move us toward creating a new interpersonal environment in which meaning systems are more integrated and inclusive. In these "lit up" moments, the patient's experience of self and other may be altered.

The process of charting a therapeutic course that is emotionally honest and open, yet bounded, may be challenging. Therapists strive to juggle the tension between openness to ethically sound, unusual-yet-useful interventions with patients, and managing the inherent anxiety stimulated by moving outside our comfort zone and deviating from standard practice.

Posing hypothetical critical incident moments, supervisees inquire, "Would you ever do X with a patient?" They are trying to discern the outer limit of what is possible or acceptable in therapeutic practice. My response is, "I can't answer that question in the abstract. It depends upon the patient, the therapeutic context, the therapeutic relationship, and what I understand is being negotiated at that moment."

Therapists may be startled by the intensity of their own affective responses to unusual requests and uncertain how best to make therapeutic use of such feelings (Bridges 1994, 2000, 2001; Ehrenberg 1992; Maroda 1992, 1999a, 1999b; Stolorow et al. 1997; Tansey and Burke 1991). At those moments they wish to construct an internal barrier to feeling, as well as an interpersonal barrier between themselves and patients. Patients' presentation of painful, personal conflicts and interpersonal dramas may be unconventional and may startle or overwhelm the therapist.

When startled, therapists may set unhelpful therapeutic boundaries as a way to manage their own anxiety.

A transsexual male wanted to attend psychotherapy sessions cross-dressed. The therapist viewed this request and behavior as a boundary violation and prohibited the patient from coming to sessions cross-dressed. This stance prematurely foreclosed the valuable exploration of this man's feelings and conflicts around being a blend of man and woman (D. Jacobs 1998). The therapist was unable to join the patient's experience and explore the layers of meaning of this behavior. This clinical boundary decision was framed as protective of the patient and the psychotherapeutic process. However, this clinical decision appears primarily protective of the therapist.

Our genuine openness to all of our patients' dissociated affects and selves allows unrestricted access to this material in the consulting room and our relationship. In the previous case, cross-dressing in sessions may well facilitate the therapeutic conversation around the experience of being a blend of a man and a woman and other dissociated self-aspects.

Therapists who are willing to construct untraditional but clinically useful boundaries demonstrate a willingness to cope with the unknown and to be influenced and educated by their patients about the therapeutic value of these events. The interpersonal and intrapsychic exploration of the meaning of these events and the associated feelings establish a context for safety. Such conversations open up space for a deeper, more intimate conversation whether or not the therapist decides to honor the request.

When confronted with an exceptional request, regardless of the valence of my initial feelings and impressions, I respond with, "Let's talk about it." This is often followed up with some version of, "Tell me what your thoughts are. How do you imagine this will go between us? What are you hoping to feel or know?" My assumption at these moments is that my patient is trying to negotiate deeply personal questions that are embedded in the manifest request. My task is to elucidate the compelling self, relational, and affective issues if I can. I direct the therapeutic inquiry toward an intrapsychic and interpersonal understanding of what is being communicated at this moment in the psychotherapy. In Chapter Three, my patient's request to bring in an erotic picture of his body is an example of how I might structure the process. I engage my patient in dialogue that I hope will lead to an increasingly complex construction of meaning and of emotional states. Such conversations facilitate a deepening of our understanding of the transference and countertransference, but even more importantly, they open space for the emergence of new forms of relational organization.

While we would like to believe that our formulation will guide how we choose to intervene in such moments, the relational reality is that it does not unfold in that manner. The therapist is rapidly shifting through and trying out a series of affective stances and self-other configurations. I adjust my position through a process of trial and error to move along toward greater attunement with my patient. As Lyons-Ruth (2002, p. 16) comments, "It is an improvisational creative process where therapist and patient try out a variety of relational moves to coordinate their interactions toward sustaining collaborative activities."

The reality is that most often we formulate such moments with our patients after we have responded. These relational moves occur intuitively and at lightning-fast speed. Unconsciously choreographed, these fitting-together maneuvers are based on our relational knowing and the particulars of the therapeutic dyad. Our patient's "answer" or subsequent response determines the assessment of the usefulness of our intervention. This may not be visible or articulated for some time. A positive response to a therapist's intervention and relational move is evident by a deepening of the therapeutic conversation. Space emerges for exploration and understanding. New aspects of the self, affective experience, or the therapeutic relationship become illuminated.

Even with an open attitude with regard to the negotiation around unusual requests, often the therapist's response may make no sense to the patient. On occasion, despite the therapist's best efforts to engage in a conversation that could lead to deeper understanding and co-construction of meaning, the patient feels wounded and feels a sense of loss. At least initially, the patient experiences the therapist as sadistic, withholding, or solely self-protective.

After two years of rewarding psychotherapy with a family I had grown very fond of, the sixteen-year-old son discloses that he believes his maternal grandmother sexually abused him as a young boy. He opts to leave the family sessions and focus on his individual psychotherapy. I continue to meet with mother and father to help make meaning of the son's statement. I imagine our sessions will help to manage the panic and rage stimulated in each parent. In a heated and anguished moment, the mother looks to me and demands that I tell her that I do not believe her son. In desperation and panic, she issues a request in the form of an ultimatum. "Tell me that you think my son is lying and that his crazy story never happened! If you don't believe me and I tell you this never happened, I will never set foot in your office again."

Flooded with feelings myself, I sense the urgency of this moment and know I must share my feelings and thinking with the family. I comment, "I see how deeply shocked and hurt you feel by your son's statements. You are pressing me to make a judgment I can't make. I believe you when you tell me this never happened, and I also hold your son's statement as his truth. It is my task to hold and honor both of these realities. I do not know what happened. It is not my place to be the arbiter of personal truths. If you like, I can help you manage the feelings that this stimulates for you and think about how to negotiate this with your family. Your son's statements must turn your world, as you know it, upside down. Perhaps I could help you sort this out." My comments did not diminish the mother's experience of being victimized and abandoned by me.

The family continued to meet with me, but the mother never forgot or forgave me for not joining her view of the situation. I imagine she was so deeply injured by her son's statements because they threatened her internal view of her mother. But her son's memories also raised painful questions and concerns about her own childhood. She could not bear to go there—not now, and perhaps not ever. This moment between us gradually sealed over but remained as scar tissue for many years. With time and other ways of being together, the injury attenuated. While we never discussed it, I came to understand that her rage became integrated with other, more gratifying aspects of our relationship. Ultimately the mother developed the capacity to allow both the "good" and "bad" experiences with me to coexist.

As in this case, sometimes we simply "agree to disagree," acknowledging that we view this differently and that each of us holds our separate reality. Trial, error, and time may also bear out that an intervention was too flexible or too rigid. Often, some time after the fact, I come to new realizations concerning what was activated internally for me that contributed to my unyielding or overly accommodating position.

Consider the following case. I lease office space to lead several psychotherapy groups. One evening as the group is ushering into the office, a woman holds up a magazine from the waiting room with a lead article on a movie star she adores, proclaiming, "I love him. I'm taking this home. I don't care what you say." I interpret this both as an indirect request and a declaration of intent. I wonder if my patient is being playful or intends to be provocative and if the group might help her see herself in this moment. Indicating that this raises an interesting boundary issue, I suggest that we discuss it in the group. The group's discussion of this event does not go very well, in part shaped by my heavy-handed participation. As testimony to just how unhelpful the unfolding conversation had been, my patient proclaims, "There is no way I'll take this magazine home now. I feel thoroughly shamed!"

After the fact, studying my internal process, I realized that when my patient proclaimed her intent to take the magazine I bristled internally. My visceral response was in part triggered by her provocative manner and in part as a result of a recent event in my own office. On occasion, patients inquire if they may borrow or keep a magazine from my waiting room. We discuss and negotiate this request. Recently, however, a publication I wanted for personal reasons was taken from my waiting room, and I was annoyed on several counts. First of all, I had plans for that particular issue. Secondly, removing an item from a waiting room without asking clashes with my personal values and stimulated my internal judge. I wondered who would take my magazine without asking.

This event and my personal values preconsciously shaped my participation in the group around this conversation. My inability to remain open, fluid, and emotionally present was compromised by my personal reaction. My feelings dominated the process, resulting in a judgmental approach to what might have been a useful conversation for this woman and the group.

Several months after the fact, I request my patient's permission to use this vignette in the book and she consents. After she reads my written piece, she turns to the group and asks if we might revisit the event and process it with her. Upon reflection, she realizes that her provocative stance set in motion a complementary set of responses. Recognizing this scenario as familiar, she recounts similar moments in other interpersonal contexts. Now she hopes the group will assist her with increasing her understanding of herself in these moments. The compelling question is how and why she leads with a provocative edge in such interactions.

The most thoughtful, well-intentioned decisions may have untoward effects and can be revisited. The hope is that through mutual exploration, the patient will come to accept the boundary as protective of the psychotherapy and her future development. Or the therapist will gain new understanding of her patient's experience and repair the error, realigning herself relationally to her patient. On occasion, some patients may be unable to negotiate such an understanding and may abandon therapy. The therapeutic relational dance always consists of trial and error, involving movement away from attunement and back to attunement choreographed by the distinct influence of each participant.

I will discuss a series of vignettes that illustrate this process, focusing on moments that routinely confuse and stress therapists such as out-of-office contact, use of touch, and gifts. An analysis of a series of critical incidents will focus on the interpersonal and intrapsychic process between and within participants, highlighting the relational and affective shifts.

REQUEST TO TAPE-RECORD A SESSION

Referred by a victim advocacy network, a woman seeking therapy following a sexually abusive therapeutic relationship with a psychiatrist phones requesting a consultation. On the phone, she tells me some of the traumatic features of her exploitative therapeutic relationship, including being abandoned by her psychiatrist after having sex. Engaged in treatment multiple times per week, the psychiatrist was also medicating her for Post-Traumatic Stress Syndrome, depression, and anxiety. Now he refuses to answer her calls and will not see her, leaving her without medication or psychotherapeutic assistance. She is in crisis and uncertain about where to turn for help. I agree to see her, and we schedule one meeting.

As I greet her, I can see and feel her terror. I imagine she rightly feels suspicious of any therapist type. After a minute or two, she informs me that she has brought a tape recorder and asks if she may record the session. I now feel distrustful myself. For a moment my anxiety focuses on my person and my worries about having our conversation recorded. I don't know her. What if I say something unhelpful? Would she possibly misunderstand my intent in a moment and use the tape for some hurtful purpose? Is this a good choice for me professionally? I respond, "Let's talk about it." I ask her, "What is your thinking about the tape recording? What purpose would it serve?" She explains to me that she dissociates and she worries that she will not be able to stay present for the entirety of our session. She would like to review our conversation later in her home when she expects she will be in a different state. It made sense to me.

With that simple request, she had shifted the power dynamic between us. Her request attempted to adjust the playing field so that she was not so disempowered in this process. I thought this was a good sign even though it stimulated anxiety for me. For a few moments, I experienced a very attenuated version of how vulnerable and untrusting she must feel with professionals now. While honoring her request moved me out of my comfort zone, I strongly felt she needed to tape-record. I hoped it might represent a positive gesture by a therapist who was willing to empower her, be open to scrutiny, and focus exclusively on her needs.

While I would like to work with her and she is willing to give me a chance, I learn she has an ongoing relationship with a victim advocate with whom I also have a relationship. I feel this is a conflict and it is best to help her find another therapist. As she interviews a number of therapists looking for the right fit, she allows me to assist her with this process of trial and error. With time, she identifies a therapist and begins subsequent treatment and the process of recovery.

Three years later, I receive a request for a psychotherapy consultation from this woman and her therapist. I agree to meet with her again. It is a pleasure to see her, and I am impressed with her gains. At the last meeting of the consultation, we are summing up and saying good-bye, and she begins to reminisce out loud about our first meeting years before. She tells me that during our initial meeting I said to her, "I am so sorry this happened to you." She continues, "You are the only therapist who ever said that to me. Thank you." I was instantly struck with the possible positive contribution and usefulness of the tape recording. At the time, mostly due to my anxiety, I had only imagined negative sequelae of the tape recording. It had not occurred to me that there might be comments on the tape that would assist her with developing a compassionate view of herself. It is possible that she might not have retained that helpful comment if she did not have the tape of the session to review as many times as she wished.

OUT-OF-OFFICE CONTACT

While many therapists are most comfortable with conducting treatment in their office setting, there are a number of occasions, some fortuitous and others planned, where we see our patients outside the office. Therapists routinely confront patients attending therapists' lectures or teaching events, or participate in patient's life-cycle rituals.

Therapy in medical settings or home visits allows access to sights and sounds and the physicality of caring that often is absent from conventional office settings (Carroll 1997). Anecdotal evidence suggests that in these settings therapists often hold themselves differently. The boundaries are by necessity more fluid and flexible. For instance, therapists may sit on a patient's bed or assist with some aspect of physical comfort or care. Our attention to the complexity of the relational meaning is important, although I expect that often these matters are negotiated nonverbally.

With some regularity, therapists attend and participate in patients' life-cycle rituals. Commitment ceremonies, weddings, graduations, exhibits, funerals, and celebrating births name some of the more common rituals. As with any other intervention, I recommend therapists carefully consider the relational context and its meaning to this particular patient and therapeutic dyad. A therapist usefully reflects upon what she hopes will be communicated or negotiated with her participation. These decisions are handcrafted to fit the specifics of the case at hand, carefully considering the full range of intended and unintended effects.

Fortuitous meetings often cannot be predicted or regulated, even if the therapist wishes that were so after the fact. While undressed in the locker room of the gym, a female colleague turns a corner and comes face to face with a psychotherapy patient. These moments happen. It is best to hold onto a compassionate self-stance. I suggest that therapists explore the patient's feelings and experience. Slowly the deeply personal and idiosyncratic meaning for the patient and the therapeutic process emerges and shifts. The fortuitous exposure of personal aspects of the therapist's life may startle both therapist and patient. A therapist may require additional support as she struggles to manage the internal disequilibrium and fully attend to assisting her patient in the meaning-making process (Ulman 2001).

Several cases where out-of-office contact was considered will be presented. I will reveal the process through which I assessed whether such contact might open up space for emerging relational possibilities.

A Good-Bye Dinner

As an energetic young therapist, I was a clinician on a locked male unit in a public psychiatric facility. While there were many organizational obstacles to providing reasonable care and treatment to my patients, therapeutic nihilism ran rampant and laissez-faire attitudes allowed me to design and engage in any creative therapeutic endeavor that I had the interest and stamina to pursue. Although the long-term staff warned me that no patient would participate, I began a weekly psychotherapy group for the men on the unit. It was a challenge to get it off the ground, in part due to the staff's negativity and resistance, but I liked challenges. Furthermore, I trusted the patients would engage with the group and me across time after they realized that I was not going to give up on them or the group.

Many of these men, aged 24 to 39 years old, had been institutionalized for many years. Forgotten by family and friends, they now were permanent passive fixtures lined up along the walls of a vacuous day hall, not interacting with a soul for days on end. With my relentless prodding, cautiously at first, the men did attend the group. Slowly across time they engaged with themselves, each other, and me. Leading this group became a highlight of my week and I suspected these men looked forward to our time together too.

After more than a year, I decided to leave my position at the hospital, which of course meant leaving these men and the psychotherapy group. While I knew leaving was the right professional choice for me, I dreaded telling these men. During the year, I felt increasingly connected to them. And to my amazement and admiration, some of the men had deeply engaged with the group and me, grieving lost lives due to the ravages of major mental illness. Their self-revelation and expression of raw emotional honesty was very moving. I sensed that they were taking great risks moving into uncharted territory. I felt honored in the group as I watched and enjoyed the unfolding and emergence of self-states and relatedness that previously had not been activated or revealed. This group had stimulated change in all of us.

The men were sad and mad at the prospect of my leaving. My departure would mean not only a loss of the group. I imagined it was quite likely that the men would lose connection with the self-states and expanded affect that had been stimulated in the group relationships. Adding to our mutual grief, there was no clinician to lead this group after my departure. As a way of honoring these men and the depth of their growth-producing connections in the group, I puzzled about meaningful ways to plant this experience internally in each member and to say goodbye. I wanted them to have a memory of the new relational ways of being and expanded affect that they had experienced in the group. I knew we would discuss this in the group, but I thought something more might be useful.

Composing a document for each group member, I outlined in what ways they had participated and what they had achieved in the group. Offering my narrative of how other group members and I experienced them, I hoped that a physical document might evoke the memory of how they felt in the group. My letter touched many of the men. I imagined for some that these letters would be treasured items. Some of the men reciprocated with a letter thanking me and commenting on my person and participation.

To my surprise, the men also had ideas about termination, including what would constitute a fitting good-bye. They proposed we go out to dinner at a local restaurant. On the face of it, this seems like an odd request, but in a milieu setting outings and activities are often part of the routine. But in the past these men had not participated in these activities. We discussed this idea at length, how they felt about it, what would be novel, challenging, or pleasing. In varying degrees they really wanted to do this, and gradually the idea grew on me too. I did wonder what this scene would look like in the restaurant, a woman in her mid-twenties dining with five men who obviously were not accustomed to restaurant dining. Would I feel conspicuously self-conscious and anxious? Maybe the men also worried about their anxiety. Most of these men had not been to a restaurant or out with a woman in many years. I wondered what feelings and memories this outing would trigger. Discussing the plan with trusted colleagues, we brainstormed about what unanticipated events might arise and thought through safety plans.

The group and I dined out at a local Italian restaurant on a Wednesday evening. The men appeared anxious and eager. As I imagined, the change of scenery, pleasing aromas, and colorful surroundings stimulated memories about other chosen meals and places long forgotten. They were appreciative of the good food and of my time with them. I felt a sense of deep grief and appreciation that I imagine they felt as well. We said good-bye.

This unusual termination event was designed by the group participants to honor the relationships with self and other that they had experienced in the group. The group allowed these men to reconnect with or to newly experience a sense of relatedness and range of affects. New ways of being with others, including a sense of belonging, emerged for many of these men. I wondered if these men in part wished to employ the group in one last endeavor to inch them progressively in the direction of the community and away from the hospital. Maybe the dining out would give them a memory to hang their hopes on. The dining out represented healthy aspects of the self reexperienced and a symbol about what might be possible. It was both celebratory and hopeful.

A Wedding

A young woman in her mid-twenties arrives for consultation in a panic. I sense that if not for the severity of her distress she would not choose to do this. Detailing the specifics of what feels like combustible and dangerous interpersonal situations, she also lets me know about her internal confusion and distress. Tentatively, at first, we work together slowly identifying how I might be helpful. I like her and admire her courage, and I sense she feels this. A well-educated, very bright, resourceful, and tenaciously determined woman, she is quite confused about powerful feelings and relationships. In time, I learn she has had a painful childhood, including leaving home as a young adolescent and making her way on the streets. A testimony to her many strengths, as an adolescent she developed protective and caring relationships with several helpful adults along the way.

We develop a close and connected relationship. She uses her time with me well to metabolize some of her earlier toxic experiences in relationships, particularly with her family. Maybe for the first time in her life, she can settle into a caring connection. Using our relationship to acquire a new template for self and other, she expands her affective competency as well. Across time, her sense of self grows and shifts, accompanied by the development of caring intimate relationships in her life. She is deeply appreciative of our relationship. I too sense how significant our relationship has been in assisting her to develop many aspects of her self, leading to significant accomplishments in her life.

With a measure of serendipity, she reconnects with a man from an earlier period of her life. With time they develop an intimate, caring relationship. When he asks her to marry him, she is delighted and almost incredulous. Proud and humbled by the developmental ground she has covered, we reminisce about her history, the details of her journey, and our history. Her thoughts turn to the details of a wedding celebration and the knowledge that she has long been out of communication with her family. It is a harsh reality, but the sad truth is that she would not want her parents to attend. So the wedding planning is bittersweet as it commingles a range of sad, painful feelings about the reality of her early family life with a sense of delight and pleasure about her current life and future.

In our relationship, I felt like a combination of her spiritual mother and a midwife assisting her in the birth of a new self and relational being. I sensed that she would like me to attend her wedding, but I felt reticent to mention this. I worried the conversation would feel awkward and maybe not go well. I wondered if my raising this would be experienced as weird or intrusive. Discussing my dilemma with colleagues, I gradually gained faith in my implicit relational knowing that she would appreciate my presence at her wedding, and I inquire, "Have you thought about me attending your wedding?" Her face lit up with a mixture of joy and sadness; "You would come to my wedding?" She cannot believe my offer and is delighted. I respond, "Yes, let's talk about it."

In the ensuing conversation, she tells me that she wanted me there but never would have ventured to ask. She felt sure it was against professional rules. Her anticipation of my refusal of an invitation to attend her wedding stimulated more disappointment than she could bear. So she never would have taken the risk of asking me.

For the next several months, we choreograph the details of my attendance at her wedding. Discussing how different aspects felt to her, we map out whom she wanted me to meet, how long I would stay, and how she would introduce me. We agree I will arrive to join the pre-ceremony gathering, stay for the ceremony, and leave before the dinner and reception. On her wedding day, she has the comfort of my presence and the pleasure of escorting me around, introducing significant others about whom I have heard so much. I have the pleasure of sharing in this developmental milestone and joyous occasion with my patient.

TOUCH

There has been a longstanding rule of abstinence on physical touch in therapeutic relationships, although all professionals do not honor it. Fosshage (2000) traces theoretical rationales against touch to the assumption that physical touch is gratifying and promotes psychosexual fixation and works against psychosexual development. In the present day, the alarming incidence of professional misconduct and the much-talked-about slippery slope of sexual misconduct leads many authors to present persuasive arguments prohibiting the use of touch in therapeutic relationships (Casement 1982; Epstein 1994; Gabbard and Lester 1995; Gutheil and Gabbard 1993). This line of thinking argues that physical contact should be avoided at all cost, as it may lead to the erosion of therapeutic boundaries and result in damaging behavioral enactments in therapeutic relationships.

In my experience, clinicians privately discuss the use of touch in their practices with trusted colleagues. A public reconsideration of the therapeutic usefulness or harmfulness of physical contact has largely been absent from conferences and the literature. I suspect clinicians develop practice styles in private around the therapeutic use or prohibition of touch. Practice styles are based largely upon many personal idiosyncratic factors, such as values, ethnicity, personal life experiences, temperament, personal treatment, and professional mentors. I will present several cases where physical contact was considered and the process through which I assessed whether touch might facilitate or stifle the therapeutic process with each person.

A Hug?

A male clinician attends a lecture I present entitled "Sexual Feelings in Therapeutic Relationships" and phones requesting a consultation. He tells me how much he enjoyed my presentation and wonders if he could meet me to see if we would be a good match. In the first several sessions he tells me that he was drawn to my energy and could tell from my lecture that I am a passionate person. Detailing the import of passion and love in his inner experience, he tells me that the absence of such love in his most intimate relationship stimulates feelings of desperation. He is hoping we might work together to assist him in securing the passionate transforming love he desires and needs. Additionally, he wonders if I might teach him "what women want from men."

I am struck with the inchoate yet palpable expectations that this man may have for me and our work based on his longings and his experience of my lecture. Immediately, I am worried that he will be disappointed. I soon realize that I am carrying his worry as well. In short order, I look very pale in the consulting room compared to my presence at the podium. As we say hello, he is worried that maybe I am not the one. Perhaps I am not smart enough, not passionate enough, and maybe not able to engage deeply with him. He worries and wonders what I want and expect from him in our relationship. Simply outlining my expectations, I include a comment about my practice being centered on conversation, a verbal treatment. I do not usually include this comment to patients, but I sensed a wish for something physical, maybe passionate, to occur between us.

During several years, I come to know him well. Although at many moments I sense that I am a disappointment to him, I also feel that he has come to trust my help and my care for him. It has been a journey. As my lengthy vacation approaches, much out of character for him, he experiences a sense of loss and anxiety anticipating my absence. During the last session, he asks if he might hug me. I was not expecting this request exactly, but on the other hand I was not entirely startled either. As I paused to think for a moment, I realize that I do not sense that a hug would be the most useful intervention for this man. I wonder if he knows why our relationship is important to him. Most familiar and comfortable with expressing deep feelings and caring physically, he is much less familiar with relationally intimate conversation. I am hoping we might discuss his feelings about being cared for and the depth of connection. Additionally, my mind wanders to his first exposure to me, and I wonder about passionate or sexual feelings. I respond, "I cannot hug you. Talk to me. Tell me what it is you want me to know with your hug."

While I am sure he was in part injured, he gives voice to his experience and tells me how much he has appreciated my care and attention. He responds, "I want to thank you. You have been more helpful to me than I imagined possible. I know more about what I want for myself, and I have a feeling of hopefulness. My relationships with others and myself have changed—especially with my family. I appreciate all your help."

I respond, "Thank you. Our relationship and work together has exceeded your ideas of what would be possible for you and us. Your sense of self has shifted. Your way of being with others, particularly with your children, has changed. You have come to count on my care and our relationship and let me become important to you. Perhaps that is part of what surprises you and gives you a sense of hopefulness. I know how much you appreciate my care and attention, and I wonder if the thank you and the hug are a signal that you will miss our time together and me."

My patient had developed feelings with and for me that he did not believe would be possible. These feelings stimulated a sense of hopefulness both about our work but most importantly about himself and his new ways of being with others. His invitation of a hug was in part a thank you and a way to cement his connection with me as we approached an absence. I too shared my feelings and perceptions about our relationship, his altered ways of being with others, and hopefulness about the future. This intimate conversation based on relational knowing highlighted for both of us that we had indeed become a good team. I hoped that having this conversation would help plant internally our relationship and his expanded sense of self.

A Kiss

For many years, I treated a young woman with a severe and unremitting major mental illness. A bright, warm, feisty woman, she displayed many idiosyncratic habits that through time only added to her charm. I developed a deep fondness for her. She was intermittently tortured with intrusive psychotic symptoms, and she allowed me to accompany her through the terror and darkness that often accompanies psychotic illness. While I often wondered if I was of any help to her at all, she seemed to appreciate our meetings and me.

As is often the case, there was a cast of care providers, both residential and outpatient, and she moved through a labyrinth of psychiatric services. Her mother was deceased, and she had no siblings. This left the family end of things to her devoted father, a highly educated and professionally accomplished man. In many such families, the grief and disappointment stimulated by a child with a severe chronic disorder challenges family relationships. Her father might have immersed himself fully in his demanding and high-status career, and nobody would have blamed him.

But he was devoted to her. He loved her and accepted her, illness and all. He was a highly valued member of the treatment team whenever we needed him. Applying his keen mind and dogged pursuit of mastery to his daughter's illness, he always had creative suggestions centered on assisting his daughter to be as autonomous as possible given the constraints of her illness. I admired him as a person, but most of all as a parent. Having him on the team enhanced my effectiveness and facilitated the therapeutic work with his daughter.

After five years of treatment, I received a call from her father, who informed me that he had an aggressive form of cancer. While he would research his options, he fully expected that he might not live long. He would like to schedule meetings to brainstorm about how and when to inform his daughter. Additionally, he wanted to be sure that arrangements were made for my continuing to care for her after his death. At first, shock and disbelief wash over me. Gradually I accept that this man who appeared so invincible was in fact dying. I schedule meetings, secure arrangements, and assist his daughter with her grief as much as humanly possible. I prepare to say good-bye to this man. I wondered and worried how my patient and her father would negotiate his dying. Her dad was a very intellectualized person who tended not to focus on the relational or affective dimensions of connections. Would he be able to give voice to those aspects of his experience as he said good-bye, I wondered.

His medical condition took a turn for the worse, and I received a call suggesting that if I wished a last visit I should do it now. Simultaneously dreading this visit and wishing to honor this man and our relationship, I visited him in his home. Slightly sedated but cognizant, he appeared very pleased to see me and stretched out his hand to hold my hand. Taking a seat next to his bed, I cradled his hand in my hand while he spoke to me.

He dispensed with the usual greeting rituals as he had something he wanted to say. He proceeded to tell me how much he appreciated knowing me and having me work with his daughter. Reminiscing about our first meeting, he shared with me his early impressions and observations of me that influenced his feelings about my work with his daughter. He is replaying a scene involving a team meeting where his daughter is "in trouble" with house staff for some minor rule infractions in a residence.

In the meeting, I am offering a different perspective and way of understanding his daughter's behavior that is less punitive and more daughter-centered. I was outnumbered, and it was an uphill trek. With tears in his eyes, squeezing my hand, he tells me, "Nancy, in that meeting you were a lioness—strong, aggressive, and determined to protect. I sensed your devotion and caring relationship with Joanie, and I knew you were good for her. Thank you. You are a lioness, and it is a great comfort and relief to know that you will help her after I am gone." Now we are both crying.

I was deeply touched by his comments and startled by the specificity of his sense of me. His comments have personal resonance because I have struggled with the lioness parts of myself, not always comfortably, and I am flooded with a range of feelings. It occurs to me that he too has felt protected and well cared for by me, in a deeply personal sense as well as for his daughter's sake. I also know that he has struggled to be the best parent possible to his daughter. Often, when confronted with yet another exacerbation of her illness, he doubted his judgment. I respond, "Thank you. I am very touched by your comments. It has been my pleasure to know you and work with you and Joanie. Joanie has been so fortunate to have you for a father. I admire you in many ways, but most of all as a parent. Your capacity to love Joanie for who she is, accepting her disability, and being genuinely helpful is amazing. I feel certain that as a parent I would not be able to do what you have done. These are very special qualities about you. You are a generous, loving man and a devoted parent." He thanks me, and we sit together quietly. After a while, I get up to leave knowing this will be our final visit. He kisses my hand, and I respond by kissing him on the cheek, and we say our last good-bye.

In this case, the patient initiated touch and I followed his lead, matching the display of physical contact. While we did not discuss it, I imagined that his grasping my hand and my holding his hand represented physical and emotional comfort. The touch embodied a display of warmth and affection and an expression of care. Touch at this moment with this man was a powerful form of communication that may have conveyed a sense of acceptance and facilitated a connection that allowed for the intimate conversation that ensued. While I might not have initiated physical contact, the use of touch with this man seemed and felt just right and facilitated a deeper connection.

Touch in therapeutic relationships holds the possibility of either facilitating or burdening the therapeutic process. In the preceding vignettes, the possibility of the therapeutic use of physical touch remains an open question to be negotiated in each therapeutic dyad at each moment in question. While physical contact is not routinely employed in my practice, I do touch on occasion, when initiated by my patient or when it makes therapeutic sense to me. There is one exception, and that is if I sense or know that a patient has erotic feelings or fantasies about our relationship and me. Under these circumstances, I do not employ physical contact, as I believe touch may exacerbate my patient's already intense feelings. I worry that touch in these cases may lead to confusion about the boundaries and the nature of our relationship.

As therapists, we need to think through the potential value and limitations of the use of touch in our practice and in each case. Touch is a potent intervention and carries the possibility of both harm and benefit. Maroda (1999a) and Fosshage (2000) report the findings of Gelb's (1982) research on touch that identifies factors that correlate with patients' positive meanings concerning touch. Factors to be considered include the following. For touch to be considered, patients' clear understanding about the boundaries of the therapeutic relationship is essential. This understanding includes the prohibition of touch when sexual feelings and erotic longings are present. In those cases, touch is contraindicated, and communication remains exclusively in the verbal arena. Other positive factors include the patients' perception that the touch is for their benefit, that they have control of initiating and sustaining the contact, and that there is a fit between touch and the level of intimacy in the therapeutic relationship and the patients' issues. I keep these factors in mind. Touch may be an intermittent form of communication in the therapeutic dyad when initiated by the patient and subjected to probing self-scrutiny by the therapist.

I find that cultural factors heavily influence patients' expectations and use of touch. In my experience, patients from Latin countries are much more comfortable with touch. In fact, Latino patients are often reassured and comforted by physical gestures as well as personal disclosures. With these patients, the use of touch seems to facilitate the forging of a therapeutic relationship, not encumber the process.

When the affect or experience to be communicated or negotiated is preverbal or dissociated, in my experience, patients may request the use of touch. This, of course, requires that the therapist be able to read and track her patient's nonverbal cues. In these cases, if the touch stirs conflict or anxiety, the patient may not notice this, or it may be difficult to put into words.

McLaughlin (1995, 2000) makes a case for the use of touch to bridge dissociative barriers and facilitate contact with otherwise unreachable patients. He reports positive outcomes. Maroda (1999a) agrees and argues for a more open attitude regarding the discriminating use of touch for purposes of therapeutic holding. She recommends thorough examination of the timing and meaning of the request for physical contact to both patient and therapist. While I have not personally employed touch "to reach" patients, supervisees have presented cases wherein touch was employed as such a therapeutic technique. These therapists touched to assist patients to overcome internal barriers with regard to particular feeling states, usually grief and sadness. These interventions designed to provoke suppressed emotions did, in fact, provoke the emotions along with a flood of other affects and longings. These therapists were surprised and startled, leading to a state of disequilibrium for both patients and therapists. Therapists were unprepared for the onslaught of arousing and destabilizing affects that led to a withdrawal from the patients as a remedy to manage threatening internal states. As a result of my limited experience with touch that is intended to provoke dissociated or suppressed feelings, I agree with Maroda (1999a) that "provoking" touch is risky.

Following my patients' lead regarding touch, I notice that their use of touch may be intermittent or occasional, consisting of handshakes or a pat on the arm as they leave my office. Sometimes patients reach out to hug me and we embrace usually around termination. I find that women initiate touch more than men, but men in my practice shake my hand, pat my shoulder, and hug on occasion. Physical contact has deeply personal and different meaning to each patient in each moment. While I often internally muse about possible meaning and I track whether it seems to facilitate or impede the therapeutic conversation, sometimes we discuss it and sometimes it just is.

As my personal comfort level around the judicious and differential use of touch expands, my practice is evolving. Often, I shake hands when I greet a new patient or say good-bye after a consultation. With regard to my initiation of handshakes, I take my cue from a nonverbal sensing between the patient and me. In general, it seems to work out, although not always. Recently, I extended my hand to say good-bye and good luck to a patient I had seen several times in consultation. She paused, looked at me, and said, "I'm sorry I can't do that." Then, she caught herself, as if reconnecting to another version of herself in the moment, and said, "I do want to shake your hand." She extended her hand, smiled, and took my hand. I received a voice message from her later in the day commenting on how proud she was of herself for shaking my hand. She had wanted to shake my hand but felt conflicted by feelings that had nothing to do with our relationship. I suspect she was pleased about her capacity to expand her repertoire of both feeling and behavior in that moment. She did not allow herself to be dominated by her history.

The vignettes I offer for consideration involve moments depicting the use of touch at the end of the hour or at the end of a treatment relationship or the end of life. While use of touch at these borders still involves uncertainty and is fraught with the possibility of positive or negative outcomes, it is a very different challenge for the therapist to touch within the hour. Furthermore, there are few accounts in the literature to guide clinicians in this domain.

I do not employ physical touch within the body of a session. In my office, the location of my chair and my patient's chair is some distance apart. This arrangement does not lend itself easily to physical contact. In McLaughlin's (2000) account of the use of touch within an analytic session, he describes the ease with which he grasped his patient's reaching hand. Clearly, he was within reaching distance. The greater challenge was how to think about the potential usefulness or iatrogenic effect on his patient and the analytic process.

In my office, my patient or I would have to rise from our chair and approach the other, a bold proposition. The seating arrangement creates a physical space that symbolizes the more compelling ethical and psychological barrier to touch. In sessions with patients, often when they are in altered states reexperiencing traumatic moments, accompanied by flooding disorienting affect, my urge to comfort physically intensifies and occupies my experience. My sense of it is that my internal experience is dominated by a strong desire to comfort my patient and not to leave her alone in her anguish.

In part due to the prohibitions around touch and in part due to my own personal discomfort and conflicts, I choose not to touch at those moments. I do worry about how my patient might experience touch at those moments. Does my wish to physically comfort arise out of a patient-centered relational approach? Or is it borne out of my wish to act, to be helpful, or to shift my internal climate as well? Most likely it represents a blend of the above. This leaves me with uncertainty about how to differentially weigh and value my patient's experience and my experience to inform my interventions.

My guiding beliefs about technique and theory as well as my character dictate my choices at these moments. My compromise at these moments has been to reach across the interpersonal space spiritually, to convey my wish to comfort physically. Shifting my physical posture, I lean forward in my chair, reaching out with a physical gesture while softening and lowering my tone of voice. I call my patient by name and offer verbal comfort. As a gesture of care and comfort, it seems to work for my patients and me. In subsequent sessions or in phone messages, patients comment on their experience of feeling emotionally held and comforted at those moments.

My temperament, personal blind-spots, and preferred theory of therapeutic action all guide my choices at these moments. Favored theoretical stances and our character shape our practice. These factors expand space for the therapeutic exploration of some material and inevitably foreclose the experience and exploration of others. In most cases, I have simply not been comfortable initiating touch with my patients or employing touch within the session. I believe it carries the risk of misunderstanding or unduly stimulating or distressing my patients. Furthermore, it does not suit me personally.

The very few public presentations I have heard involving therapists' use of touch within sessions has involved ongoing use of touch with a patient. Ongoing use of touch is yet an even more rarely disclosed and discussed clinical phenomenon. In those cases, I was struck by the dominance of the therapists' wishes or theoretical beliefs. And I was troubled by the absence of disciplined reflection and reconsideration of the therapists' preferred stance, including unintended psychological sequelae. The use of touch in those cases seemed inadequately formulated and from my perspective a misadventure bordering on hazardous.

I recognize that the unconscious use of touch, touch that is initiated and controlled by the therapist, or touch within an eroticized therapeutic relationship, may derail psychotherapy. Such touch may lead to boundary confusion or violations, or be traumatic. However, touch that is initiated by the patient, is nonsexual, and is consonant with the level of the relationship may be helpful (Fosshage 2000; Maroda 1999a; McLaughlin 2000). Maroda (1999a) comments that "non-erotic brief hugs" should be given on occasion, as the injury caused by withholding such physical contact from those who need it does harm (p. 154). As I scan back through recent years of clinical practice and survey the data regarding patient-initiated use of touch, the negative outcomes seem correlated with the therapist's refusal to honor the patient's explicit request for physical contact. A therapist's insistence that the request for touch be discussed may yield negative results as well.

Several cases come to mind in which a patient requests a hug from her therapist and the therapist refused the physical contact. Subsequently, the patient leaves the session and does not return. In some of these cases, the therapist and the patient had a long working relationship. In one case the patient was terminating treatment and did not return for the remaining session. In these cases, nonsexual physical contact was initiated by the patient and was congruent with the level of the relationship and the degree of being known. Perhaps the therapists were acutely aware of the professional prohibition against touch and experienced personal discomfort at the notion of physical contact with a patient. Or the thought of physical contact with a patient may have stimulated personal conflicts. Or perhaps the therapists wished to avoid the feelings stimulated, leading them to refuse the patients' request.

In my practice, a woman was referred to me for group treatment, and after the initial evaluative session, asks if she might hug me. As I was uncomfortable with simply honoring this request, I suggested we talk about it. This woman did not return to meet with me again. This example is complicated by the fact that I did not know this woman, and a hug seemed out of place considering the relational context. In other cases in which I have hugged a patient or shaken a patient's hand, in the next session I have sometimes invited a conversation about the physical contact. In several cases, these conversations have not gone well. My sense is that drawing attention to what may have been a social gesture, perhaps fueled by other unconscious longings, humiliated and injured my patient. In these cases, my initiating a conversation after the fact stimulated my patient's shame and self-criticism. The misunderstanding and injury stimulated by these moments remained the focus of therapeutic conversation for some time. Learning from my experience, I now most often simply allow these moments to be.

In consultation with colleagues who believe they would not initiate physical contact with a patient, I have heard numerous accounts describing moments in which they did honor a patient's request for a hug with no apparent negative effect. The incidence of professional sexual misconduct and the professional prohibition against touch leaves therapists feeling vulnerable and uncertain about the prudent and judicious use of touch. Touch may usefully communicate to our patients about our care and enduring connection.

If the therapist feels the patient and their relationship meet the guidelines previously outlined, I recommend a more fluid stance regarding the discriminating use of touch. When a patient requests a hug, particularly at the end of a session, if the therapist senses that physical contact is not contraindicated but novel in her practice, I suggest she move outside her comfort zone and consider honoring her patient's request. If, on the other hand, she is uncertain about whether hugging would be useful to her patient, I recommend that she indicate both her willingness to negotiate and her curiosity about how the patient may experience the hug. If personal conflicts, anxiety, or the professional prohibition around physical contact dominate the therapist's process and decision making, she might take responsibility for her feelings and experience. "I know you feel a hug at this moment would be helpful to you. I'm sorry. I am not professionally comfortable using touch in my professional work. Is there anything you or I might say that would be of help here? Is there a way to hug with words?" Of course, the ultimate helpfulness or harmfulness of this interpersonal negotiation and the meaning of these interactions will be determined across time in dialogue with each patient.

Fosshage (2000) argues that as therapists "we cannot afford to exclude such a powerful form of connection and communication as touch" (p. 39). I agree. However, as with any intervention and form of communication, we need to pay close attention to the layers of intrapsychic and interpersonal meaning, the accompanying affect, and our comfort level. What is being elaborated and defended against or overlooked at each moment guides our inquiry (Fosshage 2000; McLaughlin 1996, 2000; Maroda 1999b). As Maroda (1999b, p. 150) argues, a discriminating stance regarding the use of physical contact with patients is most valuable. She encourages therapeutic exploration as to "why now," followed up with a careful assessment as to the potential usefulness or harmfulness of touch at this moment with this patient.

Openness to exploring the possibility of touching or not touching at moments is most useful. Touch is a powerful form of communication that may enhance the therapeutic relationship or result in injury or misunderstanding. With an open and curious stance with regard to the differential use of touch, and with close tracking of what is being enacted and negotiated at this moment in the therapeutic dyad, intrapsychic and interpersonal meaning may be illuminated.

GIFTS

Accepting and giving gifts represents another clinical minefield for many therapists. Gifts in therapeutic relationships are overloaded with historic professional baggage around restraint and refusal. A family member who was embarking on an initial course of psychotherapy reports that her therapist said, "Don't ever give your therapist a gift. You'll never hear the end of it." I imagine her therapist was expressing his discomfort or perhaps "warning" his patient. His comment expressed his ambivalence about gift-giving by caricaturing the conventional clinical stance of "don't accept gifts from patients." Often, a therapist is confronted with a gift-giving moment and senses that the most useful intervention would be to accept graciously the gift and thank her patient. Yet the forbidding voice of internal supervisors rings loud in her ear, stimulating conflict.

When presented with a gift-giving moment with a patient, most often I accept the gift and thank my patient. Across time, after the fact, we formulate meaning as I focus therapeutic inquiry to understand what is being communicated and negotiated at this moment in the psychotherapy. Understanding the multiple relational, affective, and developmental meaning to my patient focuses my attention. What does the selection of and offering of this particular gift mean to this patient at this moment in time? What did my patient want me to know or feel? What was she hoping she would know or feel in return? Is she shielding herself from some feeling or knowing with this gift? How did she decide she wished to give a gift and how did she settle on this item? What does this gift represent for her?

The gift symbolically represents my patient and her feelings that I carefully hold and admire. I fantasize about what is the pressing communication to me. An integral piece of this process and conversation is my transparency regarding my feelings and reactions. In conversation with my patient, I include my sense of what my patient needs and wants from me at this moment. In the therapist-patient dyad, much as the mother-infant dyad, our patients comprehend our complex emotional being often through nonverbal mechanisms and can sense the therapist as person (Lyons-Ruth 1999, 2000; Lyons-Ruth et al. 1998; Sander 2002; Stern et al. 1998; Tronick et al. 1998). My response is guided by my belief that my patient knows and senses my affective state and sometimes my thoughts. These personal sensings of self and other may reorganize and expand states of consciousness and ways of being.

Repetitive gift-giving by a patient captures my attention and warrants further inquiry. As we coconstruct meaning around these moments, we are exploring what is being expressed and what is being overlooked or foreclosed. Sometimes the gift-giving becomes superfluous, or sometimes it becomes routinized practice. My patient may continue with the gift-giving until she does not need this behavioral vehicle any longer for expression of self or affect or to represent our connection.

Sometimes patients wish to leave items in my office or with me. These wishes are always interesting and therapeutically valuable to understand. The moment of the leaving and the occasion for the reclaiming is relevant. Often these items represent important pieces of my patients' developmental and relational history. Sometimes the items signify dissociated aspects of the self. Invitations for such holding may represent a wish for an enduring connection or an overture inviting other self-states into our relationship. Or such requests may express a wish to influence or control an internal or relational process.

May I Leave These with You?

A twenty-year-old woman arrives for her second session with an armload of tattered and worn notebooks. "I've been writing in these notebooks since I was eleven years old; that was a bad year. I was attacked by a dog and bullied by the girls at school. I'll leave these notebooks with you, if it's okay. I think they might help you get to know me and my history." I accept her invitation. "Thank you. I imagine these will be a valuable resource. What do you hope I will learn or notice as I read your entries?" "Oh, I don't know. I guess I want you to know that I've had a hard life and been depressed since I was about eleven. The journals tell the story." "I would be delighted to read your journals. I am also curious about how you would tell the story today." She responds, "Oh, I don't remember many of those stories. Besides, it would be too painful to talk about. Maybe later."

In this case, the invitation to read and hold her journals symbolically represented a wish to introduce memories and self-states that she could not bear to hold. Accepting the journals demonstrated my willingness to hold her traumatic memories and dissociated affects until we could talk about these experiences.

Symbol of an Enduring Connection

In another case, a woman who struggles with disorganizing separation anxiety and panic ruminates, wondering if she can trust the feelings of care and connection that she feels when she sits with me. The feelings and sense of connection evaporate so quickly after she leaves the session that she is left wondering if those comforting states actually occurred between the two of us. Or did she imagine those feelings? Across time, she comes to have more faith in the deepening of our relationship, and she takes some risks. She wonders if she might leave an object of hers in my office on loan. As we discuss this possibility and what it would mean to her, at first she focuses on it as a gift of sorts. She thinks the object is lovely and that I would like it. It would add a decorative accent to my office. All of that seems true, and of course I wonder what the object symbolizes in terms of our relationship. With continued conversation, we agree that my keeping the object in my possession represents a wish and an acknowledgment. She longs to know that I keep her with me internally as she struggles to keep me with her internally. Leaving an object with me concretizes our connection and comforts my patient until she has a secure sense of our enduring connection.

I am uncomfortable with patients giving expensive gifts or very personal gifts, such as intimate attire. While I would graciously decline such offers, I have never had to refuse such a gift. I imagine that my patients sense that such gifts would not be accepted. Rather, my patient's wish and fantasies of giving me such gifts is examined and explored. Gifts as symbols of self, as an expression of or a defense against particular feeling states, or as a gesture honoring the relational connection make therapeutic sense to me. With regard to expensive or valuable gifts, the risk of encumbering the therapeutic process is great. My feeling is that I am well paid and do not want to accept extravagant extra payment in the form of gifts. I believe it might negatively influence the process and the relationship.

On occasion I have given patients gifts, although in my practice this is a rare occurrence. Over more than twenty years of practice, I have given gifts to patients on six occasions, including weddings, birth of a child, and a forced termination. The gifts were small tokens individually chosen for the particular patient. The gift was selected to symbolize our connection and most often celebrated or marked a developmental milestone or transition.

While my professional experiences with gift-giving have been positive experiences for my patient, I know of instances when gift-giving by therapists has resulted in untoward effects. A colleague recounts a psychotherapy in which he elected to give a wedding gift, a ceramic bowl, to a patient. Although he carefully selected the ceramic bowl because he thought it was particularly lovely, his patient was upset by the therapist's choice. The gift was experienced as "not me" by the patient, representing the therapist's lack of attunement to him. But it also felt like an act of intrusion, an effort to shape or control the patient.

While the patient's negative experience and the meaning made was unanticipated by the therapist, across time with continued dialogue this event yielded significant therapeutic value. With time and negotiation, the patient was able to hold both his experiences of the gift as "not me" and as an authentic expression of his therapist's care. Both were true. For this patient, moving into an internal and interpersonal space where multiple realities could exist represented new relational procedural knowledge. The therapist structured a process that facilitated both the patient's being understood and known on a deeper level and moving along developmentally to a more dyadic understanding of this exchange.

A colleague discussed a case with me in which gift-giving created a therapeutic rupture. In this case, the therapist repeated an aspect of her personal treatment with detrimental impact on the therapy. A female psychiatrist was treating a psychiatrist of the same sex whose main presenting complaints included depression and intimacy issues. Internal conflicts interfered with her ability to make life decisions around marriage and pregnancy. After years of a mutually hard-won, good-working relationship, the patient decided with some ambivalence to go ahead with starting a family. She became pregnant.

Many years before, during the therapist's personal therapy within a warm, unambivalent relationship, her own therapist had given her a baby gift at the birth of her child. Deeply touched by the gift and remembering the very positive effect it had had upon her, she decided to give her patient a baby gift. She hoped the gift would hold similar meaning for her patient. The therapist imagined that the gift would serve as an invitation to acknowledge and deepen their relationship.

Unexpectedly, the patient was startled and frightened by the gift. It created a crisis in the therapy, threatening to rupture the treatment relationship. The patient's extreme and untoward reaction graphically illustrated that, despite her thoughtful consideration, the therapist had not fully understood the meaning of the gift-giving in terms of this particular patient. Experiencing the gift-giving as harmful, the patient wished her therapist had been able to contain her wish. The therapist's own treatment history around the positive power of gift-giving, as well as an over-identification with her patient, undoubtedly influenced her decision making.

When I have a sense that giving my patient a gift would be therapeutically valuable, initially I think through this process myself and perhaps with colleagues. If it continues to make sense to me and I believe it will indeed alter my patient's experience of self and other or confirm some new way of being, I discuss my wish with my patient. I say, "I've been thinking of giving you a gift. Can we talk about what that would be like for you?" Inviting my patient to collaborate with me in this process allows for my patient's full and deep participation. Furthermore, the conversation prepares my patient for this affective and relational experience. My aim is to diminish the possibility of my patient feeling startled and overrun by unexpected affect. Or by the experience that something is "being done to her" rather than co-constructed with her.

Within a clearly articulated treatment frame, a developmental relational approach allows therapists to play with and entertain any of her patient's unusual requests. In fact, through the explication and negotiation of these requests, we gain access to a wide range of dissociated self-states, affects, and relational scenarios. This information facilitates the deepening of our understanding of our patient's experience of self and other. Often these requests provide a window into previously unseen aspects of old relational scenarios or signal a shift in the patient's inner object world and relationship with us. A genuine openness to our patient's subjective experience and the process of interpersonal negotiation around requests opens up space for authentic engagement and moves along the developmental process. Through the clinical process of an intersubjective negotiation, our patient may expand and rearrange self-knowing, states of consciousness, and relational knowledge.

5

SELF-REVELATION IN THE THERAPEUTIC RELATIONSHIP

Balancing Expressiveness and Restraint

A developmental, relational approach that focuses on the patient's mastery of affective states and expanding her relational repertoire invites self-revelation by the therapist. The therapist's direct use of her own affective and relational experience in the interpersonal transaction is a mainstay of practice (Aron 1996; Bromberg 1998; Hoffman 1983, 1992a, 1994; Maroda 1999a, 1999b; Mitchell 1988, 1991, 1997, 2000). The mindful use of self-revelation may lead to deeply personal and transforming conversations between therapist and patient. Such dialogue expands affective consciousness, rearranges relational structures, and opens up the possibility for new meaning and relational systems for the patient.

Focusing on the interaction and transactions between therapist and patient facilitates a wide range of previously unthinkable therapeutic interventions for therapists. The therapist's subjectivity is central in the therapeutic conversation and invaluable to our patient's rearranging implicit relational knowing. The question confronting the therapist is not whether to disclose to our patients or reveal ourselves in relationship, but rather a consideration of what and when to share, depending on the clinical relationship and context (Aron 1991; Cooper 1998a, 1998b; Ehrenberg

1995; Goldstein 1994, 1997; Hoffman 1983, 1994; McLaughlin 1995; B. Pizer 1997; Stern et al. 1998).

Decisions to share feelings and personal views with patients remain a complex area of clinical practice (Aron 1991; Fosshage 2000; Lehrer 1994; Maroda 1999b; McLaughlin 1995; Mitchell 1988). Therapists who value a more fluid stance and emphasize mutuality in the psychotherapeutic process understand that use of self-revelation still requires clinical judgment. Sometimes misunderstood, a relational approach does not sanction sharing anything you feel or think with your patient. You need to evaluate your patient with relational contextual factors in mind so that you can fully assess the clinical situation and risk/benefit ratio of the proposed intervention. Any revelation will, of course, differentially open up space for some avenues of inquiry and foreclose the possibility of others.

A therapist's consideration of the developmental relational fallout of clinical choices is essential. Hopefully this data will be held as part of the relational record as she weighs future clinical decisions. The guiding parameter remains which intervention will move along interpersonal understandings and open up space for new relational possibilities. While one never knows in advance how the transaction and relationship will unfold, therapists try to imagine the relational impact of their decisions.

In a therapeutic relationship, self-revelation is a valuable tool that facilitates exploration, introduces new perspectives on the self in relationship, and conveys to the patient the possibility of creating a new, healing object relationship (Aron 1991; Cooper 1998a, 1998b; Ehrenberg 1995; Maroda 1999b; Renick 1991, 1995). Therapist self-revelation may be a helpful vehicle to make unconscious affect conscious, to identify relational dynamics that influence the treatment, or to advance the patient's development (Aron 1991; Cooper 1998a; Maroda 1999b). The therapist's self-revelation, including sharing of affects, motives, intent, and personal opinions in the context of an ongoing relational psychotherapy, is examined through clinical vignettes. When psychologically attuned and emotionally honest, therapists' revelations to patients may lead to unexpected clinical opportunities. These moments may deepen the therapeutic relationships and add a novel, growth-fostering dimension to the work.

Aron (1991) framed subjectivity in disclosure as a mindful effort to reveal to the patient an aspect of the therapist's self with the intent of opening up space for something new to be explored or understood. Cooper (1998b) articulated three therapeutic aims of disclosure, namely an effort to make something conscious that is currently unconscious in the transference; to create a new mode of inquiry and discovery; and to convey to the patient that the therapist is, or could be, a new object. Maroda (1991, 1999a, 1999b) suggested that the analyst's emotional responses to the patient are the mainstay of disclosure. Such feedback provides the patient with vital information to understand and master affect. Affective disclosures that help the patient see herself as others do are central (Maroda 1999b).

Focusing on intersubjective space and transactions invites therapists to move outside the box and improvise, employing novel and creative use of self. The relational maneuvers involved in the fitting-together process require that the therapist shift through a series of self-other configurations and select out which particular maneuvers work with this patient. Self-revelation and disclosure become instrumental in this process. With attention to building intersubjective moments of meeting and relational dialogue, new ways of being together may emerge (Lyons-Ruth 2004; Sander 2002; Stern et al. 1998).

CONSIDERATIONS

Therapists guard against excessive revelations, revelations that shift the focus away from the patient, or revelations that might harm. Monitoring the effect of such interventions on the patient and the treatment process is essential. Therapists engage in probing self-scrutiny to fully understand their own interests and influence on the clinical process (Aron 1991; Bridges 1999; Cooper 1998b; Ehrenberg 1995; Hoffman 1994; Maroda 1991, 1999a, 1999b).

Many patients report a range of feelings about the therapist's self-revelation and the impact on the therapeutic relationship (Bridges 1999; Levenson 1996; Maroda 1991, 1999a, 1999b; Wells 1994). One never knows in advance what effect such disclosures will have on a patient or the therapeutic relationship. I think of moments of self-revelation with patients as prisms catching and reflecting a kaleidoscope of different-colored light. Remaining open to the shifting layers of meaning, slowly across time therapists gather in the patients' dense experience.

A patient longs to have personal data about me, but is conflicted about asking and knowing. I inquire, "What would you like to know? What's on your mind? Ask and I'll let you know if I'm comfortable sharing the information." She responds, "I don't ask because I'm not sure I want to know. I think having the answers may make me feel bad about myself." We continue to explore how her conflict about longing to know more about me embodies her conflicts about herself. She worries that having answers will stimulate her self-judgment or feelings of disappointment. Another patient asks personal questions in the last three minutes of a session, leaving us with no time to hold and process any feelings or reactions. I comment, "I can answer your questions, but I do worry that having this information may stimulate a range of feelings for you. I wonder what that will be like for you to digest on your own." He responds, "I know. I probably will have an intense reaction, but I want you to tell me anyway." I say, "Okay, and of course we can discuss what this means to you next time." I answer his question and say good-bye. Returning to this transaction in the next session, my patient shares with me the range of his reactions to knowing more about me, including his appreciation of my answering his questions. My honoring his request in the last minutes of a session gave him the sense that I experienced him as sturdy. It conveyed my faith in his capacity to manage whatever came up for him around this data. My feelings in this moment stimulated strongly positive feelings about himself. This experience offered him a new sense of his own sturdiness and his capacity to tolerate potentially disruptive, negative feelings on his own.

Patients may be reluctant to report the full range of feelings and reactions to a therapist's revelations (Levenson 1996; Wells 1994). To enhance the therapeutic value of self-revelation, the therapist must initiate the conversation and be prepared to work through the full range of a patient's feelings and reactions (Ehrenberg 1995; Levenson 1996; Maroda 1991, 1999a, 1999b; Wells 1994).

Fortuitous or spontaneous revelations by therapists hold the same potential for the full range of beneficial and untoward effects as do intentional revelations by therapists. The interpersonal and intrapsychic effects of any fortuitous revelations on the patient, the therapeutic relationship, and the therapeutic process are revealed through careful therapeutic inquiry. A therapist focuses on elucidating the multiple meanings of the event to the patient. Ultimately, the range of positive and negative effects of unintentional disclosures is discovered mutually in the therapeutic dyad across time as therapists gather in the full array of self and affective experience.

A SPECIAL CATEGORY:
DISCLOSURE OF SEXUAL FEELINGS

Disclosure of sexual feelings and fantasies with patients is an area of ongoing controversy, although in large part the debate seems to have gone underground. Several years ago there was a flurry of both published material and conferences focused on erotic feelings in therapeutic relationships. The controversial question of whether therapists might ever usefully disclose such feelings and thoughts to patients is debated. In her paper "Love in the Afternoon," Jody Messler Davies (1994a) describes an analysis in which she disclosed sexual fantasies to her patient, precipitating a groundswell of debate on disclosure of erotic feelings in treatment relationships. Davies represents the analytic point of view that includes the possibility of the disclosure of the erotic to patients, arguing for the therapeutic value of such exchanges. Gabbard (1994b, 1996) and others view therapists' disclosure of the erotic as a potentially damaging and inappropriate intervention.

At a Boston Psychoanalytic Institute and Society conference on erotic material in analysis, George Fishman (1999) commented that he believed that male therapists and erotic feelings were akin to "a fox in a chicken coop." They simply could not be trusted to screen out their instinctual and libidinous strivings to clearly assess and determine if or what erotic disclosures might be therapeutically valuable to which patient under which circumstances. For those reasons he believes such disclosures are never appropriate. For those of us who have a less instinctual perspective on male sexuality, it still does seem like a minefield, particularly when we are continually confronted with those among us who engage in professional sexual misconduct with patients.

The conventional wisdom and prudent stance is that the treatment process and the patient may be harmed by therapists' declarations of sexual feelings and fantasies. At times, therapists' experience intense, even urgent sexual feelings for patients. At those moments, therapists' sexual feelings may best be used silently in formulating the meaning of these feelings in the treatment process and relationship. A protective stance advises any therapist who is convinced of the benefit of frank disclosure of sexual feelings and fantasies to patients to seek consultation before any such disclosure. Frankly, we simply do not have enough data about the usefulness of such interventions, and the risks seem very great.

As a consultant to therapists who either have made personal disclosures of sexual feelings or fantasies towards patients or are considering such disclosures, I am impressed with the powerful tug of enactments driving the wish for disclosure. In some cases, the patient therapist felt intensely attracted to her personal therapist. She longed for her personal therapist either to be mutually attracted to her or to acknowledge the attraction and erotic tension that was co-created and mutually felt. The therapist patient desperately needed acknowledgment from her therapist about the existence of the intense feelings and longings between them that were mutually experienced but inadequately formulated. The absence of acknowledgment and affirmation either through silence or denial left the therapist patient feeling enraged and caught in a double bind. This scenario may well resonate with earlier relational experiences of self and other.

I imagine the treating therapist was ashamed and troubled by the erotic feelings. The treating therapist's shame and guilt prevented her from fully experiencing this mutual, co-created experience with her patient. Unable to formulate these affects and the relational experience with her patient, the therapist emotionally left the relationship, clamping down on her subjective experience and on her patient. The residue of this experience stayed with the therapist and cast a shadow on her experience of erotic feelings with patients. Enacting an aspect of her personal therapy, the therapist projected her personal experience onto her patient. The therapist's compelling unconscious desire to rewrite this scenario from her personal therapy led her to declare sexual feelings or fantasies towards her patient. In the consultations, I was most impressed with the patients' use of sexuality to communicate a wide array of non-sexual feelings and self-states that felt too shameful to hold. These patients were seeking to manage shame and self-loathing around dependency longings, not primarily issues of attraction. Sexual material protected these patients from experiencing the depth of a wide range of other longings and conflicts.

In these cases, the therapists' disclosure of sexual feelings and fantasies to patients seemed misguided and unhelpful. The patients' experience and developmental issues were deeply misunderstood. The therapists' capacity to differentiate between self and other was compromised. These therapists became too closely identified with their patients as self, collapsing analytic space and perspective.

The accounts from these therapists around their own treatment experiences represent the legacy of our collective professional phobic dread and the historic mishandling of these issues and feelings in therapeutic relationships. Historically, a common experience for patients struggling to negotiate sexual feeling states in therapeutic relationships was to feel injured and blamed by their therapists. Unable to bear these feelings and associated self-issues, therapists dissociated personal feelings of erotic longings and shamed their patient, turning the sexual feelings into grief and anger. Therapists are vulnerable to misunderstanding or mishandling these complex therapeutic issues with their own patients if negative or harmful experiences around erotic and loving feelings occurred in their personal therapy.

INTRODUCING NEW PERSPECTIVES ON SELF IN RELATIONSHIP

Often, patients live with positive and negative self-distortions and transference schemas that do not serve them well. They do not see themselves accurately. An outside, discrepant opinion about self in relationship is invaluable to many patients. Patients may lack self-observation skills and feel injured or committed to their view even when it does not work well in relationships.

> A profoundly lonely and isolated woman presents for psychotherapy requesting help with relationships. While she does not understand the course of relational events, she knows that she has a pattern of alienating and offending others. Unaware of how she contributes to these dilemmas, she also is exquisitely interpersonally sensitive. She presents a current dilemma with her husband around a painful interaction and is seeking my assistance. The patient has scripted a response to her husband that I feel is mean-spirited and self-focused. I worry her response is likely to prompt a sadistic response in return. I offer my view to my patient by commenting, "I see how hurt and angry you feel with your husband. You long for more of his understanding and attention. Would you like an outside opinion about what might be useful here?" The patient agrees. I continue, "I know you are hurt and angry and may wish to hurt in return, but I feel your greater wish is to have more of your husband's compassionate attention. I'm afraid if you present your side in this fashion that you will most likely receive an angry, hurtful response in return. While it is, of course, your choice, I don't think that would be helpful to you. When you are hurt and angry, it is very difficult for you to imagine how the other person feels. A conversation that owns your disappointment and his feelings as well is hard to come by. Maybe we could help you figure out a way to present your side that would increase your chances of feeling understood."

Our patients need and want our assistance with those feelings and dilemmas that they cannot see, understand, or shift on their own. Often patients have no internal models for how to negotiate their wishes and needs with another. Patients rely upon us to assist them in acquiring new procedural knowledge in relational domains. Often, these teaching and modeling moments involve therapists' self-revelation and disclosure around affect and relational experiences. Our view of the dilemma at hand is helpful. Despite the inherent injury involved in having developmental deficits or relational dilemmas highlighted, when an outside perspective is offered in an instructive and compassionate manner, patients may be very appreciative. Patients need our emotional and observational feedback to see themselves the way that others do and to expand their experience of self and other (Aron 1996; Maroda 1991, 1999a, 1999b; Renik 1991; Stern et al. 1998; Tronick 1998; Wilkinson and Gabbard 1993).

COUNTERTRANSFERENCE DISCLOSURE OF DISOWNED AFFECT AND RELATIONAL CONNECTION

The use of countertransference disclosure around therapeutic impasses has been well documented in the literature (Darwin 1999; Ehrenberg 1992; Gorkin 1987; Maroda 1991, 1999a, 1999b; Tansey and Burke 1989, 1991). When patients have trouble identifying their inner experience or disown intolerable self and affective states, the therapist acts as a container or receptacle for the patient's dissociated self and affective states (Ogden 1994; Wilkinson and Gabbard 1993). In these situations the therapist offers countertransference disclosures as a means of beginning to identify and explore material that may be unconscious or otherwise would be unavailable to the therapeutic process (Gorkin 1987; Maroda 1991, 1999a, 1999b; Tansey and Burke 1989, 1991; Wilkinson and Gabbard 1993).

An isolated young man with a chaotic inner world, who is sensitive to abandonment and shamed by the intensity of his feelings, denies that he has any feelings or reactions about my impending absence. From my perspective, it has been a year of therapeutic gains as my patient's sense of self has increased along with a deepening of the relational connection. I worry that this disruption in connection may be particularly traumatic for my patient. Several weeks before my leave-taking, my patient reports that suicidal ideation has returned. He worries about his safety. After addressing safety concerns, I turn my attention to understanding the suicidal ideation. I wonder if these symptoms are related to my upcoming vacation. The patient remains unable to identify any feelings.

Given my patient's inability to identify or articulate his feelings, I disclose my feelings and observations to him. My aim is to facilitate exploration and help identify dissociated affects that may place him at risk. I comment, "I have felt very close to you, very connected to you this year. You have come to count on me and have let yourself become very involved with our work and me. It feels to me that you allowed me to care for you, to help you in new ways. I imagine my vacation will be difficult and will stir a range of feelings and reactions, including sadness and anger. I'm sorry my absence will make things harder for you. I will miss you while I am away and will think of you."

The patient listens silently and then turns his attention to a painted figurine in my office. He wonders if the object is a recent addition, as he has never noticed it before. The patient continues by sharing observations about the figurine, stating, "What an angry face!" I comment with energy, "His therapist is going on vacation." My patient looks at me and smiles with affirmation.

I took a risk here, a preformulated, calculated risk. I presumed that my subjective experience of increased closeness and connection represented the state of affective attunement between my patient and me. I held the disowned, shameful affects around connection and his longings. The sadness and anger represented my subjective experience, and it also imitated my patient's experience. My patient's association to the figurine's angry face and his smile after my comments confirmed my hypotheses. The point here is that I understood my experience as mutual and co-created in the therapeutic relationship although not named by the patient. My disclosure was an attempt to assist the patient in identifying and naming his affective and relational experience. An attitude of openness and inquiry is essential at these moments. The patient is invited and expected to agree, disagree, and revise the therapist's comments and disclosures. The therapist's disclosures can be viewed as editorial comments that the patient may play with or discard. In any event, the conversation becomes part of the permanent relational record for future examination.

THERAPIST'S VULNERABILITY

Therapists who are confused about the nature of therapeutic action and ambivalent about self-exposure and vulnerability may retreat from open, honest conversations with patients, including self-revelation. Sometimes the more comfortable position for the therapist is to remain protected behind a professional veneer. A protective stance, however, forecloses the experience of intense affect, deep conversations, and self-revelation with our patients (Bridges 1999; Ehrenberg 1992, 1995; Maroda 1999a, 1999b; Renik 1991; Stolorow et al. 1997). While therapists continually self-reveal and disclose in therapeutic relationships, authentic moments of meeting with patients often involve a heightened discomfort or a sense of disequilibrium for the therapist (Ehrenberg 1995; Lyons-Ruth 2000; Renik 1991, 1995; Stern et al. 1998; Ulman 2001).

A willingness to share your view in therapeutic relationships means allowing your patient to see you, to know you, and to engage in what may feel like a personal conversation that has a therapeutic intent and purpose (Aron 1991; Ehrenberg 1995; Maroda 1991, 1999a, 1999b; McLaughlin 1995; Renik 1991; Stolorow et al. 1997). While self-revelation is vital to facilitating shifts in our patients' internal structures and altering ways of being, it may be fraught with anxiety for the therapist. As therapists reveal feelings and aspects of themselves, they too feel vulnerable and exposed to the scrutiny of patients (Bridges 1999; Maroda 1991, 1999a, 1999b; Renik 1991). The therapist's comfort level is at stake. Furthermore, there is no way to know how the meaning of a revelation will shift across a therapeutic relationship and changing affective states. For these reasons, therapists are often reluctant to share personal material unless a trustworthy rapport has been established. Even then, there is no guarantee how the patient will hold the disclosure. Consider the following vignette.

MEANING OF REVELATION SHIFTS WITH RELATIONAL AND EMOTIONAL STATE

A patient in a long-term psychotherapy that has helped him transform his sense of self and quality of life is struggling with the logistics of managing a stressful career and a household with young children. Having grown up in a desperately poor family and now in an affluent position, the patient has no historic models for how one organizes such a life. Over the years I had assumed valuable developmental and emotional roles with this patient. I functioned as a psychological guide, mentor, coach, mother, father, and sibling. My patient wants to know how I manage similar logistics in my life as he tries to construct a model that might work for him. After exploration of the meaning of the request, I share personal information about how I manage such logistics, including hiring household help. The patient appreciates this information and finds it helpful.

Several years later, after a divorce that decreased the patient's standard of living, he is again stressed by the logistics of managing all the responsibilities in his life. He is enraged at his situation and at the people around him. He experiences the loss of his marriage and the decrease in his standard of living as a descent into the deprivation of his childhood. In a moment of anguish when he feels I had misunderstood him and become "other," with contempt he snarls, "How could you understand? Look at your life. I don't have household help like you do. You can't possibly understand!"

I felt hurt and angry and regretted that the patient had this personal information. Years earlier, at the moment I had shared this information, it felt like a personal gift from me to him. For a moment, I spiritually left the patient and internally focused on my feelings of injury. I wondered about the usefulness of my earlier disclosure. I felt stunned that a personal revelation that had seemed so helpful years earlier was now being used in the service of the patient's rage and despair. I felt attacked personally. My patient's resentment and anger at his impoverishment and my ambivalence about being privileged stimulated my self-judgment and inflamed my sense of vulnerability. Realizing that revelations are filtered through the lens of shifting emotional and relational states, I had a new sense of what was potentially at stake with personal revelations and the excruciating degree of vulnerability involved.

As therapists we like to believe that we decide how to best use ourselves in the therapeutic moment based upon the patient's developmental and relational needs. However, with regard to revelation of personal data, I believe a therapist is more likely to disclose when she has a certain modicum of trust in her patient. This trust includes faith in her patient's capacity to manage affect.

Despite the therapist's best effort to engage in an authentic process of negotiation and exploration about the meaning of a therapeutic self-disclosure, it is often not possible to know in advance how the revelation will affect the patient and the treatment process. Time and further conversation may be needed for the therapist and patient to discover mutually the multiple meanings and effect of the revelation.

As in the previous vignette, the meaning of the revelation may shift across time, filtered through the patient's ever-changing inner landscape. Trial, error, and time may also bear out that a revelation was harmful or unhelpful or some blend of both. The most thoughtful, well-intentioned self-revelations may have an untoward effect. If processed in the treatment dyad, even untoward effects may ultimately be very valuable in deepening the understanding of a patient's experience and feelings. On occasion, some patients may be unable to initiate such a conversation with the therapist. The responsibility for examining and reexamining the meaning and effect of the revelation rests with the therapist.

SELF-REVELATION IN THE SERVICE OF REPAIRING INJURIES IN THE THERAPEUTIC RELATIONSHIP

When a therapist crosses a boundary or injures a patient, self-revelation is often a necessary part of the process in understanding the internal and relational meaning to the patient and repairing the connection. As in the following case, an important piece of repairing the injury with a patient is my taking responsibility for my contribution.

A young woman comes for treatment of her depression, anxiety, and profound sense of isolation. An accomplished professional, her complaint is that she has no life outside of her career. She is not one to complain, but if she allowed herself to reflect on her life she would say she was unhappy. While deeply lonely, it is hard for her to have my undivided attention. Often the patient struggles to stay connected to herself and identify how she wishes to use her session.

After several months of treatment, the patient arrives for her session and begins to update me on her thoughts and feelings. I notice I am half-listening as my thoughts are pulled to my own concerns, a lecture I am to deliver after this therapy appointment. Catching my mind drift from my patient, I refocus. As I observe my patient's face, I notice my patient's expression has shifted into a mask of sadness. I wonder and ask my patient, "What are you feeling now?" The patient does not have any idea. I continue, "You look very sad." The patient bursts into tears, weeping too vigorously to speak and then comments, "I'm boring. I think I'm boring you." I wonder silently if the patient noticed my attention drift away.

Rather than impose my hypothesis on my patient's experience, I ask her, "Is there something I said or did that made you think I was bored?" The patient responds, "It was your behavior, the way you looked." I now believe that my patient did notice my attention shift, and I feel it is important to share this information with her. I disclose that, in fact, my attention had wandered for a moment. "I was not bored nor do I find you boring. A matter in my own life captured my attention for a moment. I wonder if that was what you noticed. I was internally occupied and not focused on you." The patient affirms she had noticed.

I did not find this woman boring; rather, I experienced this woman as very bright, thoughtful, and earnest, with a refreshing sense of humor. I did wonder if my internal reverie mirrored a similar state for her which ever so slightly pulled her out of connection with me as well. I apologize, "I can see my divided attention has hurt your feelings, and I'm sorry. I was the cause of the distraction; it was not about you. But I wonder if this reminds you of other moments in your life." I inquire about the patient's assessment of herself as "boring" and wonder if she has had that feeling before in relationships.

While I imagine that my preoccupation with the upcoming lecture moved me out of the relationship, I also wonder what, if anything, about my patient's presentation today facilitated my movement away from the therapeutic dyad. I hold these thoughts in reserve as I gather more information. As the session continues, we explore new material about the patient's private experience of the self and her feeling shame around "having nothing to say" when she is with people. It becomes clearer that this patient's deep-seated internal doubts and negative attributes cloud her assessment of herself in relationships. She has a distorted view of how others perceive her. Later in the session, I comment, "This conversation helps me understand why you are so reluctant to place yourself in social settings. You are very sensitive and perceptive of others. Perhaps you notice others' reactions but do not have enough data to know whether someone's reaction is about you or not. Without data to the contrary, you hold yourself responsible for others' feelings and reactions. It's easy to understand that you might want to protect yourself from that injury and disappointment."

My self-revelation in this case was in the service of repairing an error, an empathic failure. It also may have attenuated a small enactment. While I know that simply informing my patient that she is not boring will not alter the patient's self-perceptions, I want to establish a collaborative stance with my patient. My hope is to invite her feedback and encourage the free expression of discrepant experiences. Emotional honesty is important in all psychotherapy relationships, especially with patients who are uncertain about who they are or how they feel. With this revelation, my response provides a model of emotional honesty for the patient while challenging her prevailing self-views. If my patient comes to feel that I am firmly planted on her side, she may, across time, become curious about her participation in the boring scenario.

MAKING CONSCIOUS UNCONSCIOUS AFFECT AND RELATIONAL PATTERNS

One of the most challenging dilemmas for therapists is to choose to address directly the patient's objectionable affects or character traits that offend or alienate. While therapists worry about how to sensitively begin a conversation about a patient's effect on others, including the therapist, these moments are often invaluable to our patients. Hopefully these conversations begin the process of the patient increasing her self-awareness and building mutuality in relationships.

A thirty-year-old, single man with a childhood history of sexual abuse has been in psychotherapy for two years for treatment of his anxiety and depression. This man feels fundamentally alone in the world and unworthy of care. Despite his terror of becoming dependent, he develops a close, yet ambivalent attachment to me. As buds of hope about himself and his future begin to develop, my vacation approaches. My patient develops severe separation anxiety, a deepening of his depression, and rage at me for leaving him. Humiliated by the depth of his feelings and attachment, he refuses all help around my absence.

When I return, the patient is flooded with murderous rage and recounts the suicidal despair and hopelessness he barely contained during my absence. During sessions, he recounts his sadistic night and day dreams about harming me. My patient's rage and sadistic entitlement are difficult for me to witness and hold.

Clearly, the patient's distress is a reaction to my absence and the feelings this loss stirs for him. Trying out multiple hypotheses of how to formulate exactly my patient's affective and relational dilemma, I share my best guesses with my patient. I hope to offer containment and convey to my patient my understanding of the depth of his shame and anger. I offer, "My vacation came at a very bad time, just when you let your guards down and were counting on me. My leaving you must pick the scab off the feelings you had as child when your mother violated you." Subsequent sessions are devoted to exploring his childhood experiences of helplessness and injury.

The patient settles momentarily. However, his rage does not abate, and his fantasies turn to sadistic sexual torture of me. After recounting a particularly brutal dream in which I am recast as a bug that the patient dissects and then destroys, he turns to me and asks, "Aren't you ever afraid someone will physically hurt you in your office? You're not very big." Without the benefit of internal or external supervision, I respond almost reflexively to feeling so threatened: "If you physically hurt me, our relationship will be over. I will not work with you and I will press charges." I feel as if the patient crossed a boundary, an emotional boundary. His comment implied a threat of crossing a physical boundary. I know my patient has the fantasy of behaviorally reenacting his childhood trauma in the consulting room with the patient cast in the role of perpetrator and me as a helpless child.

My comments startle my patient, and he responds: "I would never physically hurt you." My patient and I explore the intrapsychic and interpersonal meaning to him of my disclosure. While the sharply defined limit I set initially hurt the patient's feelings, it offered containment and facilitated the exploration of new material and affects. Sharing my feelings and thinking with my patient, I comment, "I appreciate your telling me that, and I'm sorry I hurt your feelings. That was not my intent. I'm not sure you appreciate fully the strength of your feelings and how you affected me. Your comment about physical harm scared me. Frankly, I think it was also an indication that you were frightened by the intensity of your anger and fantasies. We need to find a way to discuss your anger and hurt that doesn't scare you or me." The patient shares his knowledge of how he disconnects from painful affect and then is startled when he confronts the affect mirrored by another.

Subsequent sessions focus on his malignant inner view of himself and belief that he would be violated and ultimately abandoned in any relationship. I share my view. "You have felt deeply cared for in our relationship. I imagine it's disorienting and scary. Feeling cared for prompted feelings of wanting to flee or destroy the relationship. It's hard to trust that this relationship could be different." We agree to monitor the cycles of connection and disconnection from his internal affective experience as well as in the therapeutic relationship.

In this vignette, my sharing of my affect and understanding of the clinical dilemma were vital to reestablishing psychological safety and deepening the therapeutic conversation. In addition, my patient needed to hear from me about my resonance with his inner experience of terror and of losing control and losing me. The needed intervention was a statement of how this patient affects me. This negotiation facilitated a shift in his self-state and made new domains of exploration possible. The identification and exploration of my patient's feelings and issues helped differentiate our connection from past relationships. I conveyed to my patient the possibility of developing a caring, connected relationship with me, even when he was angry.

My self-revelation provided containment and deepened the interpersonal and intrapsychic understanding of feelings and the relationship. While my many formulations were reasonable best guesses, it was after the disclosure of affect and intent that my patient and I mutually formulated the intrapsychic and relational meaning that informed the next phase of the work.

DEEPENING THE THERAPEUTIC CONVERSATION AND EMERGING RELATIONAL KNOWLEDGE

At the beginning of treatment, a woman in her late fifties was unable to have any positive feelings about herself or others. She could not hold any memories of pleasant events. She was filled with confusion, deep uncon-scious longings, self-contempt, and rage.

After many years of psychotherapy, she told me how much better she felt about herself and that she felt close to me. She would like to give me a gift of appreciation, a thank-you, for all my help. She had in mind a piece of inexpensive, cherished jewelry she had purchased many years before from a symbolically significant country. She, however, only wanted me to have the gift if I liked the item and would wear it. At first, I was startled by this unusual overture, but I managed to focus our efforts toward the ex-ploration of my patient's feelings and wishes. I hoped to better understand what she was longing for, or perhaps protecting against, with this overture. What did this particular gift signify for her?

Initially I felt anxious and then annoyed. This overture felt like a setup for my patient to be injured or for me to be twisted into an unacceptable position. What if I disliked the gift? Knowing my patient was easily in-jured and how important my reactions were to her, could I declare dislike? Perhaps the therapeutic stance was to feign liking the item and mindfully wear it once or twice a year? I did not think so. Clearly, I had little idea what conflicts and affects were being negotiated here. I needed more in-formation from my patient.

I was worried about the likelihood of this turning out badly and hurt-ing my patient or the therapeutic relationship. I found myself feeling less and less like this was receiving a gift and more and more like I was tip-toeing through a minefield. Sharing my worries and concerns openly with my patient, I wrestled with how to make meaning of this request. I knew my patient so appreciated my opinion and affirmation. "How would you feel if I disliked the jewelry? Would you feel that I disliked you?" How would she feel about herself and me if we had different tastes in jewelry? Would she feel diminished or hurt if I was different from her in this way? My patient seemed to be risking a degree of vulnerability and intimacy she had never allowed herself to experience before in a relation-ship. She experienced herself as sturdy in this process, self-knowing, and certain about her wishes and longings. She wanted an honest response. I, on the other hand, felt anxious and confused about what would be ther-apeutic in this case.

I was now filled with feelings that were discrepant from my patient's stated experience. My experience and feelings occupied my inner process, although I consciously tried to stay with my patient. I was not convinced that she would not be injured, despite her insistence. Furthermore, I had trouble imagining speaking the truth when I could not imagine the possibility of any positive outcomes. As a way to protect myself, I remained unhelpfully fixed on the request as a reenactment of the faulty affective attunement and attachments my patient had known as a child and experienced throughout previous psychotherapy experiences. Perhaps this was a repetition of childhood disappointments with needed others?

Luckily, my patient did not give up on me and was undeterred despite my limitations. She knew intuitively what she needed from me, even if she could not articulate these feelings and issues so that I understood. Pointing out my unwillingness to have a truly open dialogue, she accused me of not taking responsibility for my own feelings. She commented, "You can't take the heat, so you're leaving the kitchen." She smiled, warmly poking fun at my dilemma.

She accurately perceived something about me. What was I avoiding? Perhaps I was afraid of feeling vulnerable, of disappointing or angering her, or of closeness in the treatment relationship? My openness to one set of transference-countertransference experiences was a resistance to feeling a set of others. I did not fully understand my countertransference reaction but was willing to be influenced and educated by my patient. Moving outside one's comfort zone is a critical dimension of this process. I felt the gift was a therapeutic opportunity that would add a new, unknown dimension to the therapeutic relationship. With uncertainty, I agreed to view and discuss my patient's gift.

Comforted by my faith in my patient's intuition and my belief that an authentic response and conversation were developmentally important to her, I disclosed both my worry and my best guess of what this interaction might mean. I shared my concerns about injuring her, my faith in her intuition, and a belief that whatever the outcome we would negotiate the feelings together. After viewing the jewelry, I offered these comments: "They're beautiful, lovely, a work of art. It's easy to understand why you cherish these pieces. They represent the history and craftsmanship of a country, which I know mean so much to you. While I think they're beautiful, I would never wear them. Thank you for sharing these with me. How is it for you to hear me say this?" With trepidation I offered her the opportunity to engage in an exploration of the interpersonal and intrapsychic meaning of this conversation and event. While my patient may have been disappointed by my response, much to my surprise and relief, the disappointment seemed minor. During the weeks to come she and I continued to explore the meaning and significance of this event and their relationship.

Through sustained engagement with this material, I came to understand that this overture was an invitation for more intimacy in the therapeutic relationship. My patient needed and longed for an emotionally honest response. The interpersonal and intrapsychic exploration of the associated feelings and the meaning of this event to the therapist-patient dyad established a context for safety that opened up space for a deeper, more intimate conversation. An honest, authentic response allowed my patient to embrace fully the affirming, admiring feelings and experiences she and I had shared previously. If I was to be deeply trusted as an observer and allowed to influence her inner view of herself and interpersonal view of others, she needed to know that I was emotionally honest with her and not simply being "therapeutic." Having worked with me twice weekly through many years, my patient had a good sense of my style and taste in clothing and jewelry. She had chosen an item that she must have known would be other than my style. After the fact, I imagined that my protracted period of uncertainty and the ongoing relational exploration combined with my genuine worry about the meaning of this event were developmentally valuable.

With my patient's help, I "structured a process that opened up the moment and allowed for deeper conversation, which enabled the patient to begin to discover and utilize resources in herself that she had never known" (Ehrenberg 1995, p. 24). This exploration helped her to shift her idealization of me and to understand she had something important to offer her own treatment and me. This therapeutic conversation consolidated my patient's experience of me as a new object, one that differed from her early childhood objects. It enhanced my patient's experience of the self as worthy of worry and admiration. The effort to study the meaning and qualities of mutual experience in this moment created the space and conditions for an intimate encounter. It would have been impossible without openness to self-revelation and a willingness to rely upon the expertise of my patient (Aron 1996; Ehrenberg 1992; Hoffman 1994; Maroda 1991, 1999a, 1999b). As this vignette illustrates, the creation of meaning in a therapeutic relationship is a shared achievement, and emotionally vulnerable moments hold the potential for significant relational shifts (Ehrenberg 1992; Hoffman 1983; Lyons-Ruth 1999; Sander 2002). Moments of meeting that embody authentic relational transactions between therapist and patient tax the therapist but offer a rich opportunity for expanded affective and self-knowledge.

RELATIONAL EXPANSION OF AFFECT AND SHIFTING SELF-STATES

Remaining attuned to our patients and assisting them with the regulation of affect requires shifting through a range of self-other configurations in the service of fitting together. The opportunity to replay old relational scenarios is accompanied by the possibility of acquiring new self and relational experience. Self-revelation is central to this process and facilitates movement into new intersubjective space.

> A patient phones for an appointment after a lengthy break due to business travel and holidays. While he has deeply engaged in our work during several years, meetings have been punctuated by many absences secondary to frequent business trips. I sense these absences provide him with a much-sought-after break from the heavy emotional lifting in our sessions. As we review our schedules, we try on many possibilities and nothing fits for many weeks. As I gaze at the upcoming month or so, I am reminded that I am overbooked with extra teaching commitments. I worry that finding time will be extra challenging. With my schedule in mind, I comment, "This is difficult." I am aware of wanting to find an appointment in a timely fashion because I enjoy working with this man. But I also find that the breaks seem to interrupt the deepening of our work. As a last resort, I offer a time that I can make available by shifting something else. We agree to an appointment time.
>
> As we begin the session, my patient wants to return to our scheduling conversation and wonders why I commented, "This is difficult." He continues, "I don't want you to think you're not important. My absences are not an indication about how I value our relationship or the work. I have a demanding work schedule. I feel I will be involved with you and this work for a long time, and it does not matter much if we take breaks due to scheduling. I know the next time I see you we will pick up where we left off, and it's all right with me.

I don't understand why you said this is difficult. It's not difficult for me. It's simple. I accept that due to your schedule and my schedule we will have scheduling problems. It's okay with me."

I sense mounting energy in my patient's voice and wonder if he felt my comment was a statement about him and perhaps heard it as, "You are difficult." Does he feel injured or criticized? I inquire, "Did my comment feel personal? Did you feel I was saying you were difficult?" He responds quickly, "No, I didn't think it was about me, but I didn't understand it." I believe my patient is accurately disclosing his experience, but I hold my theory in reserve. I continue to worry that I have hurt his feelings and stimulated his internal self-critic. I wonder. I continue, "I do wonder if our not meeting stimulates other feelings for you." His energy continues to mount, and now I also sense his frustration with me. He comments forcefully, "It really is very simple. I've explained it to you, and that's how I feel about it."

Now it seems that my patient feels backed into a corner with me or by me and occupies a frustrated, maybe angry, space, making it increasingly difficult for him to gain access to other versions of himself. At this moment, I feel as if he cannot see me, and there is no space for my perspective in this conversation. I wonder if this is how he felt with his father, a demanding and critical man.

I comment, "It's not that simple from my view." He immediately responds, "I'm telling you it's that simple." I match his energy and encourage him to stay connected to me. "Stay with me here, try to hear me out. I'm saying it's not that simple *for me*. Let me tell you what I was thinking and feeling during that conversation when I commented, 'This is difficult.'" He pauses. "Okay."

I continue, "As I looked at my book, I couldn't see an open spot for many weeks, as I have taken on some additional teaching. I know you don't mind, but I do feel it works best when we meet on a regular basis. I didn't want to have to wait so long before we met again. It's not that I wonder whether you can manage, as I know how competent you are. I think I missed you while you were away, and perhaps my wanting to meet sooner was about our recent absence and my missing you." I sense an immediate shift in his mood and self-state. His voice softens and he says, "That's nice. I'm pleased you missed me. I appreciate your telling me." I continue, "I think I was missing you, maybe that's why I felt so determined to meet sooner." I continue, "Do you have any of those feelings?" "I wouldn't use the word miss, but I appreciate you," he replied.

I say, "Tell me what you appreciate." "Well, there are several things. I feel emotionally held by you, and I appreciate that. I feel that you are on my side, and I like the way you talk to me. You always say things to me in a way that I can listen to and hear. I know that you are interested in me, and you care about me. You are the only person who says to me, 'Tell me more.' You want to know me." I respond, "I do. It's good to know about the qualities in our relationship and with me that you value. Thank you."

I say, "Do you know what I missed about you?" He responds, "I would like to know." I respond, "I'd be happy to tell you. I value your sharp mind, can-do spirit, your determination, and courage to wade into uncharted waters. Your willingness to disagree with me, to stake out your feelings and opinions, and to engage in dissent is a special quality about you." He responds, "Really, I can't believe you said that. No one has ever said or felt that way about me before. In fact, most women I've been involved with would say they dislike that quality about me. Why did you say that? I don't understand that."

I respond, "I feel that dissent and disagreements are relational gifts, of sorts. When we encounter conflict or disagreements, I learn so much more about you, about what matters to you, about your deep feelings, and I believe it forges a closer relationship." Pleased and surprised by my response, he comments, "You know, that's what I like about you. You are so strong. Disagreement is okay with you. You can take care of yourself."

In the next session, we return to this exchange, and I tell him, "I have been thinking about our last conversation. There was a moment between us when I felt strain and a threat surrounding our non-sameness. Seems there was something around the non-sameness that was frightening or threatening. Did you notice? What do you know about this?" He responds, "There was a personal difference. Reminds me of conversations with my sister where I would dig in my heels. It continues to improve but there is something about difference. I was relatively pleased with our conversation. Glad I didn't go downhill fast with my anger. When I think about my business, difference has been hard for me, but I'm getting better at it. Not so black and white anymore."

I respond, "I wonder if this dilemma around difference leads back to your dad. He could be so threatening and coercive. He was a man who could not tolerate difference or dissent and demanded you submit to his will, insisting that you were wrong or bad. It's so complex. I think something about difference frightens you, and your anger is your way of managing your fear." He responds, "At work sometimes, I feel silently controlled or like I'm silently controlling another. I don't even know when I'm doing it until after I've done it. It's hard to let go of control." I comment, "Must feel dangerous on some level. Feel you need to be in control to protect yourself or manage your fear. It's why you worry about feelings with us. Feelings become stimulated in our work that you weren't expecting. It's hard to control."

He responds, "I don't want to be afraid of something. I want to be brave, but it's still there. I am afraid. It's amazing, though, when *you* say something it's not so bad." I respond, "Accepting that you're scared sometimes is not so bad." "Yeah, like saying I'm scared. All that energy keeping it out of my awareness." He chuckles with acceptance. I say, "It's not so bad, knowing something scares you." He continues, "I wonder what it will be like when I'm not scared. It's funny how much has changed since we started. How much better I feel about myself, know what I'm feeling, and manage my feelings. I still feel in the shallow end of the pool."

Reworking issues around dependency, feeling vulnerable and angry, my patient replays familiar relational sequences around how difference is handled. As we approach our non-sameness, I feel him move into this old, familiar space that he knows well from his relationship with his father. While we have previously discussed his childhood experiences with his father, replaying this scenario between us is new. The danger and potential risk of rupturing our connection and my being experienced as an adversary is very real and present.

In these sessions, my comfort and freedom with spontaneous expression and self-revelation facilitates my patient's regulation of affect. It also helps shift his self-state while focusing on our interaction. In the therapeutic relationship, we are beginning to outline what internal obstacles and childhood relational procedures interfere with his capacity to know himself and to be in connection with others. Difference in relationship and the affects stimulated for him will be an area of ongoing exploration. Can there be difference without denigration? Can he hold his experience and stay in connection with another? Can multiple realities exist? Does he have to follow the family model of dominate or be dominated? Can he bear to know his inner feelings?

Following my lead, he moves from a psychic space where he felt under siege and threatened to the possibility of holding and negotiating a difference in our relationship. Through our sustained attention to both internal processes and the transaction between us, we move from a reenactment of affective relational scenarios from his childhood to a more inclusive and collaborative state. Feeling my warmth, sturdiness, and care for him, even during negative affect and dissent, was a new experience and a comfort. Transparency concerning my internal process and revealing my feelings and thoughts only increased his openness to his internal process and the possibility of a new relational experience.

An intersubjective relational model that views the therapist as a full participant in the co-creation of the therapeutic relationship and as an active player in the unfolding of the inevitable "crunches" of an interpersonal psychotherapy relies upon a therapist's self-revelation and disclosure. A therapist's direct use of her own affective and relational experience with the patient is a means to deepen therapeutic exploration and understanding, introduce alternate interpersonal perspectives, and make conscious material that will foster self-development. Often, these moments are experienced as high-risk, high-gain opportunities and carry the potential for derailing or significantly deepening the therapeutic relationship. There is much at stake. The accumulation of such repetitive relational transactions holds the promise of rearranging a patient's sense of self and internal structure (Lyons-Ruth 2000; Sander 2002; Stern et al. 1998; Tronick et al. 1998).

Employing self-revelation, therapists should remain patient-focused, rely upon the patient's resources and expertise, model emotional honesty, monitor the influence of self-interest, and share their view of the clinical relational experience. The therapist's use of humor, improvisation, and creativity in the service of developing a new interpersonal context is central. Therapists usefully initiate exploration of the multiple intrapersonal and interpersonal meanings of such revelations and the effects upon the patient. Moments of self-revelation that injure or rupture the safe, familiar intersubjective environment may be revisited and repaired with concerted effort. Therapists' self-revelation and disclosure are essential, valuable therapeutic tools that deepen the therapeutic conversation and relationship and lead to unexpected possibilities for patient and therapist alike.

6

THE ROLE OF SUPERVISION AND CONSULTATION IN MAKING MEANING AND KEEPING ONE'S BALANCE

Supervision and consultation play essential roles in assisting therapists in their capacity to hold and formulate intense feeling states and maintain their therapeutic balance. Support, technical assistance, and a fresh view are invaluable resources in order to maintain our balance during periods of arousing and destabilizing affect and powerful enactments. Absence of supervisory attention to these issues or access to consultants leaves therapists exposed to the risk of engaging in destructive behavioral enactments or developing practice styles that abandon the patient and stifle the psychotherapeutic process.

A model of individual supervision and consultation is proposed for therapists and therapists-in-training, focusing on the therapist's relational understanding and management of intense feelings. How the supervisor sets the frame, formulates learning goals, and introduces and manages the emergence of personal feelings will be considered. Helpful processes include paying attention to therapists' safety and comfort, assuming an educational rather than a therapeutic stance, focusing on skill development and acquisition, and providing therapists with a cognitive framework for understanding affect. Shame and self-consciousness may be diminished through the supervisor's willingness to assume a self-revelatory stance, including sharing personal mistakes and making the process transparent. Ethical supervision is embedded in a clearly articulated supervisor-student relationship that monitors misuse of power and boundary crossings, yet is capable of deeply personal discourse.

With inadequate preparation for managing overwhelming and startling affects, therapists run the risk of being over-identified, engaging in destructive behavioral enactments, or developing restricted practice styles that abandon the patient and stifle the therapeutic process (Gabbard 1994a, 1996; Maroda 1991). Supervisors and consultants are in a unique position to assist trainees and seasoned therapists with these boundary dilemmas (Gabbard and Lester 1995; Jacobs et al. 1995).

Relational supervision that addresses therapists' understanding and management of personal feelings in themselves and in their treatment relationships is valuable. This, of course, includes discussions of the construction of clinically useful and ethically sound supervisory and treatment boundaries. I offer one view of how to integrate personal conversations concerning supervisees' feelings, experiences, and issues into a supervisory process in a manner that is clinically and educationally useful, respectful, and self-enhancing for experienced therapists and trainees. In this chapter, I employ the term "trainee" to designate both therapists in training and licensed therapists seeking supervision.

PERSONAL ASPECTS OF SUPERVISION

Despite years of professional debate on how personal supervision should be, opinions still vary widely on the optimal point of balance between focusing on the supervisee's management of the case and exploration of the supervisee's thoughts and feelings (Freidlander et al. 1984; Jacobs et al. 1995; Lakin 1991). Supervisors and consultants may be uncomfortable with the personal aspects of supervision and feel ill equipped to focus the supervisory dialogue on the supervisee's issues, feelings, or person.

Many supervisory dyads make a clear and conscious decision to restrict discussion to the patient's data and the supervisee's management of the case in an effort to protect the therapist from the risk of boundary confusion between supervision, personal therapy, and the experience of shameful feelings. Others advocate for a strict avoidance of the supervisees' personal data because they believe inadequate separation between supervision and psychotherapy results in supervisees' alienation and because the supervisory hour is the primary arena wherein supervisees experience shame and guilt (Allen et al. 1986; Alonso and Rutan 1988; Freidlander et al. 1984; Robiner 1982). Possible harm to supervisees is always a concern. The absence of clear, shame-free models of supervision that include personal dialogue may shape and limit how supervisors conduct supervision.

Dyadic, relational, intersubjective theories require that we pay attention to the inner experience of the trainee-therapist as well as the patient (Aron 1996; Hoffman 1994, 2002; Maroda 1991; Rodolfa et al. 1990; Roman and Kay 1997). Psychotherapy supervisors and trainees must be able to openly discuss these feelings and processes in an interpersonally safe, shame-free, and educationally sound manner in order to advance the psychotherapeutic process.

FRAMING THE SUPERVISORY RELATIONSHIP AND PROCESS

Therapists learn to increase affect tolerance through experience, personal treatment, and supervision (Alonso 1985; Jacobs et al. 1995; Thorbeck 1992). Because of the power differential between supervisor and trainee and the ubiquitous shame and almost phobic dread surrounding the discussion of "objectionable" feelings in supervision, the supervisor must initiate the conversation and set the tone for such discussions (Bridges 1998; Lakin 1991). Alonso and Rutan (1988) believe a great deal of shame and guilt in supervision flows from the supervisor's confused notions of where to position herself. Just as many supervisors are uncertain about what is appropriate and how personal supervision should be, so too are supervisees. Often this shame, guilt, and confusion are passed on to the supervisee. Supervisors may combat trainees' shame and anxiety by clearly articulating the parameters of the supervisory conversation. Supervisors may establish an interpersonal climate of openness and safety where sharing personal feelings and experiences may occur by offering the following frame for the supervisory relationship and work.

> Clinical work often evokes strong feelings including attraction, sexual arousal, rage, disgust, and grief (among others) in our patients and ourselves. These feelings are both expectable and unavoidable. Recognition and therapeutic use of these feeling states are invaluable in therapeutic work. Often, these feelings signal important information about our patients' development and relational difficulties, about ourselves, and the therapeutic work to be done. Supervision is a place to sort out the nature and meaning of these feelings when they arise to guide your clinical work. I trust as these issues arise in your clinical work, you will bring them to supervision. I will be happy to share with you my own experience struggling with these issues as we feel it's useful. I neither want to intrude nor do I want you to struggle without assistance with these complicated feelings (Bridges 1998, p. 218).

These comments are an invitation to the trainee to discuss personal issues as they impact on clinical understanding, management, or educational goals. If the supervisor sets the teaching frame to include discussion of personal feelings and issues when they arise, the likelihood of a constructive experience increases.

Supervision needs to be a trustworthy, shame-free milieu wherein intense affect, personal experiences, complex identifications, and relational dilemmas are a central focus of discussion. A supervisory focus on personal issues is intended primarily to assist the trainee with competent, compassionate care of patients and management of boundaries. While such focus may, on occasion, help identify personal issues that would benefit from psychotherapy, it is not intended to help trainees work through these issues.

Supervision focused on personal feelings and issues is not a substitute for personal treatment. All practicing psychotherapists need to have personal treatment as a vehicle to a deeper understanding of the psychotherapeutic relationship and process, to increase affect tolerance, to increase self-knowledge, and to work through personal issues.

HELPFUL PROCESSES AND STANCE

Supervisors need to monitor and strike a balance between personal conversations that are clinically useful and educationally sound and those that ultimately feel intrusive or disrespectful (Jacobs et al. 1995). The following guiding parameters may assist supervisors as they negotiate boundaries and discuss personal feelings in the supervisory dyad.

Creating shame-free learning milieu. Normalizing a trainee's shame, powerlessness, and self-consciousness about not knowing, being a trainee, and struggling with personal, painful feelings in treatment relationships helps create an interpersonal environment where self-exposure, risk-taking, and clinical curiosity are possible (Bridges 1998; Jacobs et al. 1995). We, as supervisors, want trainees to bring their relational dilemmas with patients, shameful mistakes, and confusion to us.

Use of self as demonstration model. Therapists at all levels benefit from senior clinicians' examples of how they managed unbearable affect, how they muddled through and ultimately made sense out of inchoate feeling states. The supervisor assumes a self-revelatory stance in supervision with regard to these clinical issues and consciously uses herself as a demonstration model for the supervisee when indicated (Bridges 1998; Jacobs et al. 1995). At carefully chosen teaching points, a supervisor shares shameful mistakes, humiliating clinical moments, and examples of countertransference dominance with attention to how to understand and manage these dilemmas. With attention to the supervisees' level of comfort and particular learning needs, a supervisor who is willing to expose his or her work and relive incompetent and overwhelming clinical moments thus gives supervisees hope about their own development and an invaluable model for mastery.

Learning contract. Useful clinical supervision begins with a careful assessment of the trainee's educational strengths and learning edges and a clear articulation of the supervisor's expectations. Clearly establishing the boundaries of the supervisory relationship helps create safety and a framework that allows both participants the freedom to share inner feelings and experiences (Lakin 1991). The logistics of the supervisory relationship, including length, time, and frequency of meetings and how clinical data will be presented, are outlined by the supervisor. Because many trainees report unsatisfactory supervisory experiences, a discussion of previous supervisions, focusing on what has and has not been useful, is indicated (Allen et al. 1986; Hutt et al. 1983). Any particularly harmful or useful styles of supervision are noted and discussed.

Next, clearly articulated learning and supervisory goals are discussed. As the trainee articulates what exactly she would like to learn and the supervisor shares what exactly she feels she has to teach this particular trainee, they mutually identify and agree upon areas that will be the focus of their efforts.

An important part of the initial contract is an invitation from the supervisor for any and all feedback from the trainee about how the work and relationship are progressing (Allen et al. 1986; Hutt et al. 1983; Robiner 1982). Specifically, the supervisor recommends that the trainee inform him or her of any unhelpful exchanges or interactions between them. By inviting the trainee to be an active, evaluative partner and suggesting open discussions, the supervisor models that difficult topics are to be included in supervision. Successful supervisory work is collaborative. Invitations to include the discussion of personal reactions in supervision and in treatment relationships set the stage for the possible inclusion of personal feelings and experiences in supervision to advance educational goals.

Educational, not therapeutic, models. Supervisees usually want to be mentored, treated as colleagues, and not be intruded upon personally. Unwarranted or unsolicited discussion of a supervisee's person or issues is at best unhelpful, and at worst damaging. Such discussion has no place in supervision unless the supervisee's functioning and care of patients is impaired. Supervisees value supervisors who give feedback in a straightforward manner, accept mistakes, and encourage them to experiment and take reasonable risks (Allen et al. 1986; Alonso 1985; Lakin 1991). While supervisees value an emphasis on personal growth issues over teaching of technical skills, they want to be treated respectfully and not viewed as clinical subjects (Allen et al. 1986; Lakin 1991).

The most helpful stance in supervision is an educational stance (Jacobs et al. 1995; Lakin 1991). This stance and focus in supervision are on skill development and acquisition. Providing information for mastery, offering demonstration models, normalizing the inherent learning difficulties, and empowering supervisees with a cognitive framework for understanding the process represent essential supervisory tasks. Such a stance offers trainees a personal mentoring experience. Supervision builds upon the trainee's life experiences and innate talents while confronting clinical professional areas that need attention.

Discussion of personal feelings and experiences may be useful when done with a clinical educational focus (Bridges 1998; Jacobs et al. 1995; Lakin 1991). The intent of such conversations is the development and acquisition of particular clinical skills or attitudes to increase therapeutic effectiveness. In such a model, supervisors notice and attend to the trainee's misunderstanding or avoidance of particular affects and remain empathetically attuned to moments of affective overload. Often, these represent important teaching moments.

Attention to interpersonal safety and shame. By paying close attention to the trainee's sense of privacy, level of exposure, shame, and interpersonal comfort, it is possible to conduct a clinically useful conversation. The supervisor needs to be aware of the trainee's feelings and process and inquire, "Is this tolerable and useful?"

Openness to the unique aspects of trainee's experience. Setting the supervisory frame to include discussion of personal feelings and experiences is an invitation, not an ultimatum. While trainees need to understand that the discussion and understanding of feelings in treatment relationships are essential to ethical care, during the training years they develop comfort and competence with this aspect of clinical work at their own pace. Each trainee must develop a relationship with a trusted and wise colleague, supervisor, or consultant with whom such clinical conversations may occur. Understanding and managing intense affect, resultant therapeutic issues, and boundary dilemmas are a career-long task for all clinicians (Gabbard 1996; B. Pizer 2000; S. A. Pizer 2000).

The level of discourse and intimacy in the supervisory or consultative relationship is co-constructed by each dyad, taking into consideration special sensitivities of the supervisee. It is not a requirement for every supervisee to discuss personal feelings with her supervisor. Because of personal developmental issues, poor match with the supervisor, or other nonspecific issues, trainees may not feel safe despite the supervisor's best efforts to create safety. Some trainees may not be able to discuss personal feelings and experiences in supervision. These include trainees with a cognitive learning style, those who have not yet experienced personal treatment, and those who for idiosyncratic reasons are particularly afraid of affect or self-exposure. In these instances, a cognitive frame of reference for understanding affect in treatment relationships and the supervisor's use of self as a demonstration model are valuable (Bridges 1998; Jacobs et al. 1995; Thorbeck 1992).

Cognitive framework for understanding affect. Trainees need reassurance and permission to experience and explore all feeling states (Alonso and Rutan 1988; Jacobs et al. 1995; Thorbeck 1992). Communicating to trainees an abiding faith in their learning process and the normative developmental phases of mastering these aspects of psychotherapy is valued. Discussion with a trusted supervisor may be of great benefit to the trainee as she attempts to assess the clinical situation. These consultations assist the trainee as she sorts out the meaning of these feelings to the patient, to herself, and to the treatment process. Supervisors provide support and a cognitive framework to guide trainees as they explore the multiple meanings of these affects by focusing on understanding what important information their feelings signal about the patients' development and relational difficulties, about the clinician, and about the therapeutic work to be done.

Constructing clinically useful therapeutic boundaries. One's clinical formulation and consideration as to what intervention will move along interpersonal understandings and open up space for new relational possibilities shape boundary decisions. The fiduciary relationship and codes of ethical conduct as defined by each discipline represent the guiding parameters for care. Within these parameters there is room to move, and each therapist constructs clinically useful boundaries dependent upon the therapist's formulation, personal style, needs of the patient, and issues being negotiated therapeutically.

On occasion, supervisors may focus meaningfully on a trainee's personal issues by identifying a need for personal treatment, as illustrated in the following vignette.

IDENTIFICATION WITH GRIEF

A capable male psychology intern presents a long-term psychotherapy patient who is challenging for him. The patient has recently been diagnosed with a debilitating chronic illness and is overwhelmed with anger and a sense of loss. As the intern presents his process notes, it is clear that he is having a particularly difficult time staying with the patient's affect.

With a clearly articulated educational contract that allows the supervisor to begin exploration, she notes that he seems to stray away from his patient's experience and expression of profound sadness and grief. Had he noticed or is he aware of those moments in the session? He had not noticed, but now that the supervisor points it out, he readily recognizes that this is so. The supervisor comments, "It is painful and difficult to stay present, bear witness, and experience the depth and rawness of our patient's pain. Frankly, it's simply too painful, at times." She hypothesizes that this is a manifestation of his inexperience, a normal developmental process, and expects he will get better with practice. During several weeks of supervision, they continue to discuss strategies to assist the intern in increasing his awareness of his process and to focus on the exploration of affect with this patient.

Despite the focused supervisory assistance and numerous efforts identifying obstacles, the intern is unable to shift his style to stay with his patient's sadness and grief. Both student and supervisor wonder if there is an unidentified component at play because the intern is able to be affectively present with other patients. The previously agreed upon educational alliance and learning goals enable the supervisor and trainee to develop hypotheses of why this is so challenging. The supervisor asks the intern, "What do you think is going on? Are you afraid of something?" The supervisor's guiding hypothesis was that he was worried about joining the patient's affect and being overcome with grief. She continued to explore the trainee's experience and his view of the patient by posing the following questions. "Is there something special about this patient that makes it difficult? Does it pertain specifically to the affect of grief? Are you worried about feeling too sad or grief-stricken with this patient? Are you trying to control your inner experience and have to move away from the patient's experience to do so?"

The supervisor checks in with the trainee by asking, "Does this feel okay? Does this feel useful?" The intern affirms that he wants to understand and master this. He thinks it relates to a piece of his history and shares that his mother died suddenly when he was eight years old. As a child, he was a capable overachiever, and neither he nor his family members received treatment.

After naming this piece of his history, the trainee realized his grief-avoidance stance with this patient was related to the early death of his own mother and his reservoir of unresolved grief. He was afraid that if he joined his patient's affect he would unleash his own grief, which would incapacitate his professional self. His unresolved grief and identification with this patient compromised his work with her.

At this point, the supervisor restated her professional belief that all clinicians need their own personal treatment. She commented, "It's a deeply personal decision about when one enters treatment. All therapists have issues to sort out that become stirred up by clinical work. If it's not grief work, it's revisiting a relationship with a family member who may suffer from an illness or some other challenge. It is commonplace for clinical work to highlight our personal issues. Your issues with grief are getting in the way of your clinical learning goals. I feel certain that when you choose to enter therapy, it will help you with your grief. You may have your own resources, but if you would like I could give you a list of potential therapists who are not affiliated with this training program."

The supervisor did not raise the issue of personal treatment again, nor did she inquire about whether he had begun treatment. She focused on the trainee's clinical educational goals and care of patients. Across several months, she noticed that her trainee's work with Ms. S. had become less restrictive and affect-avoidant. When the supervisor congratulated the intern on his good work and clinical development, he shared that he had begun psychotherapy and found it clinically and personally useful. The intern was now able to bear his anxiety and grief and help his patient with her sadness and grief around her illness. He and his patient went on to do a deep, sensitive piece of work around loss and mourning.

In this vignette, the supervisor assumed a therapeutic role for a short period to help her trainee identify what issues were preventing him from reaching his educational goals and taking good care of his patient. In a limited sense, the supervisory relationship took on a quasi-therapeutic nature in the service of increasing his clinical effectiveness through enhancing his understanding and therapeutic use of affects (Jacobs et al. 1995; Lakin 1991). The supervisor did not focus primarily on personal issues, but instead used this trainee's personal data to advance his professional development, clinical work, and learning goals.

FORMULATION OF SEXUAL FEELINGS

A male trainee experiencing sexual feelings for a female patient presents the case in supervision. The patient, a 28-year-old, single, socially isolated, depressed, and physically attractive woman, presented for treatment after the death of her mother. The trainee experiences this patient as very likable and in desperate need of care. Since her mother's death, the patient feels frightened and childlike, alone in the world. After several sessions, the trainee is startled by his sexual fantasies about this patient. During sessions, as the patient shares details of her anguish and despair, he is troubled by his fantasy of embracing her and kissing her on the lips. The trainee is ashamed and embarrassed by these feelings and wonders what they mean.

The supervisor comments, "It's brave of you to let yourself know about these feelings and to bring them to supervision. It's hard. Often, these feelings are so troubling and confusing for clinicians that they prefer not to acknowledge them or to keep them private out of a sense of shame. Often, these feelings are important diagnostic clues that give us information about our patients' inner world and developmental issues, about the state of the clinical work, or about ourselves" (Bridges 1995). "If we assume that these feelings represent a projective process, how might we begin to understand what is symbolically being communicated here. Our task is to formulate and try on multiple formulations and hypotheses of possible clinical meanings. If we view these fantasies and feelings as a metaphor, what is your patient trying to tell you about her wishes, fears, history, and the like? Once we arrive at a working formulation, we will decide what clinical interventions may be useful."

In this vignette, the supervisor attended to the trainee's self-esteem as well as the care and management of the case by praising the trainee and providing technical assistance. It is important that the supervisor acknowledge the trainee's feelings of shame and embarrassment and the courage it takes to expose oneself and request needed assistance (Bridges 1998; Jacobs et al. 1995). These supervisory moments are crucially important not only to the management of the particular case and the trainee's self-esteem; they also represent a potential template for future consultations around troubling, shameful feelings. Supervisors want to take every precaution to make sure these teaching moments are helpful both to the trainee and to the management of the case, so that trainees will replicate these consultative experiences across their professional lives.

A clinician's struggle with intense, conflicted identifications may interfere with clinical decision making and be presented in supervision, as in the following case.

POINTS OF IDENTIFICATION

A therapist presents in supervision a difficult clinical decision with a patient and her confusion about how to proceed. The patient, a young adult woman with major mental illness, has been treated by this clinician for many years. Across the years, the therapist has developed a relationship with the patient's mother, the only family member who has been an important ally in her daughter's treatment.

The mother is diagnosed with pancreatic cancer and is expected to die within a year. Understanding that her mom is dying, the daughter's mental status deteriorates rapidly. She becomes acutely psychotic and unable to keep appointments, her self-care diminishes dramatically, and she is no longer able to function at her previous level. It is decided the daughter's best care option is to be admitted to a residential treatment facility many miles away.

The therapist brings a seemingly straightforward dilemma to supervision. Should she terminate with this woman and plan a good-bye process now, as she feels the new facility is too far for her to travel? Or should she try to continue to meet with her at the new residence and terminate if this does not work out? The mother has let the therapist know she hopes she will continue to care for her daughter after her death.

As the therapist presents the dilemma, she begins to sob, a heart-wrenching wail. The supervisor waits, then says, "You're very upset. What's the dilemma you're facing here?" The supervisor wonders silently if the therapist is grieving the mother's dying, maybe identifying with the daughter's impending loss, or experiencing her own sadness about saying good-bye to her patient. The therapist comments, "I know what I want and need to do, and that is to terminate. I don't understand why I'm so upset." The supervisor asks, "Do you want to talk about it?" The therapist responds, "Yes." The supervisor wonders out loud, "Are you feeling a sense of divided loyalty?" and begins by focusing on the weight of the mother's request that she continue to treat her daughter. The supervisor refers to the intimate conversations between spouses when one is gravely ill and concerned about the continued care of children, a deathbed conversation if you will. She comments on both the intimacy of her relationship with the mom, as if she is a family member, and the sense of burden she must feel.

The supervisor wonders, "Does the daughter or this scenario remind you of someone? It's not important that you share the data in supervision with me, but it would be important for you to figure it out for yourself. Perhaps something deeply personal is being played out in this treatment. Your distress is a testimony to your personal strength and capacity to allow yourself to engage deeply. You will figure this out."

The therapist comments she thinks she knows what it is. As a child, she felt trapped with caring for her mother, who had psychiatric problems. It was a major and painful developmental step for her to separate from her mother and family as a caretaker. Now she feels like a child again trapped with a mentally ill mother as her patient's mother is dying. "How can she desert this woman?" is the emotionally wrenching question. Yet she also knows it is not possible logistically for her to travel the distance.

She thanks the supervisor, commenting that the conversation has helped her identify the source of her distress and the complexity of the clinical relationship to this mother and daughter.

In this vignette, the therapist used the supervisor to name and locate the origin of her distressing affect precipitated by intense conflicted identifications. Acknowledging the disorienting effect of overwhelming affect, the supervisor offers support and multiple levels of engagement. She invited the therapist to decide whether or not to share and to explore these feelings in supervision or not.

INTENSE TRANSFERENCE/
COUNTERTRANSFERENCE STATE

A female therapist presents a complicated treatment case in supervision. The patient, a 32-year-old single male, presents with depression, suicidal ideation, and a childhood history of sexual and physical abuse that precipitated a series of foster care placements. An intense attachment and transference to this therapist developed as the patient used the treatment relationship to understand his difficulties with interpersonal relationships and managing intense feeling states. After nine months of treatment, the patient presents a boundary management dilemma in the form of an unusual request that breaks the treatment frame. The patient wants the therapist to read a favorite childhood book to him while the patient sits in the therapist's lap like a child. The therapist is overwhelmed with conflicted feelings and confusion about where to set the therapeutic boundary. The supervisor normalizes the therapist's feelings of being overwhelmed and confused and offers a relational, developmental frame of reference to assist the therapist in formulating this dilemma and what might be clinically useful.

After formulating the case and arriving at what seem like useful boundary maintenance interventions, the therapist remains visibly distressed. The supervisor notices and comments, "You seem upset." The therapist responds, "I'm very upset, but I'm not certain that I should discuss my feelings with you in supervision." The supervisor inquires,

"How do you think about that question?" "I don't want to be inappropriate, and I'm not sure how you would feel or think about me if I speak openly about my upset." The supervisor reassures the therapist that the discussion of her personal feelings is appropriate if she feels comfortable, and together they monitor issues of privacy. She would be happy to try and help her identify the source of her distress with this patient if she likes, but it is the therapist's choice. The therapist continues by sharing details of her personal history that match and overlap with this patient's early history of trauma and abandonment. She feels so identified with the patient's anguish and longings that she does not trust her clinical judgment. She worries she will be overly accommodating out of feelings of over-identification with this patient.

The supervisor praises the therapist, "I admire your courage in being so open to yourself and in supervision. Our work with patients is often deeply personally evocative. Inevitably, clinical work intersects with our own history and most vulnerable issues. I know in my professional work that having a safe place to sort out these dilemmas has been crucially important. It does get easier with experience and practice, but I continue to get startled from time to time and seek consultation." The therapist reveals that she has taken her dilemma with this patient to her personal therapist. The supervisor recommends that they work on noticing and differentiating between her personal and professional responses to this patient. Supervision may assist in keeping track of this difference and focusing on her patient's needs and dilemmas.

These moments of overwhelming affect, conflicted identifications, and boundary maintenance dilemmas predictably occur across one's professional life. Even though personal treatment is highly recommended for all clinicians, not every moment of intense, confusing, conflictual identification in therapeutic relationships can be relegated to personal treatment. Sometimes therapists simply need a shame-free, trustworthy relationship to sort out such enactments and affect in order to get back on track. Supervision and consultations need to address the needs of trainees and experienced therapists at these moments.

The capacity to formulate and manage intense feeling states is a fundamental clinical skill necessary for all practicing therapists and essential to the construction of therapeutically useful clinical boundaries. Intense feelings and the resultant complex aspects of clinical work present lifelong clinical challenges for clinicians. Therapists need trustworthy, professional mentoring relationships wherein they can safely sort out shamefully held co-created countertransferences, the tug of complex identifications, and knotty relational dilemmas with patients. Whether the experience of intense, often taboo, affects in therapeutic relationships will be held by therapists as shameful secrets with the inherent risks of technical mishandling or behavioral enactments or fruitfully discussed in supervision is central to clinical outcomes.

Supervision in the training years may provide the template for a trainee's lifelong handling of such matters. With attention to setting the supervisory frame to include personal feelings and experiences, respectful, clinically useful, supervisory dialogue that addresses trainees' understanding and management of personal feelings may occur. Assuming an educational rather than a therapeutic stance, focusing on skill acquisition and development, and providing trainees with a cognitive framework for understanding affect and construction of therapeutic boundaries are helpful components. Supervisors who judiciously reveal their own experience of struggling with and mastering these skills may be valuable role models.

REFERENCES

Allen, G., Szolos, S., and Williams, B. (1986). Doctoral students' comparative evaluations of best and worst psychotherapy supervision. *Psychology: Research and Practice* 17(2): 91–99.

Alonso, A. (1985). *The quiet profession: Supervisors of psychotherapy.* New York: Macmillan Publishing.

Alonso, A., and Rutan, S. (1988). Shame and guilt in psychotherapy supervision. *Psychotherapy* 25(4): 576–581.

Applebaum, P. S., and Jorgenson, L. M. (1991). Psychotherapist-patient sexual contact after termination of treatment: An analysis and a proposal. *American Journal of Psychiatry* 148(11): 1466–1473.

Aron, L. (1991). The patient's experience of the analyst's subjectivity. *Psychoanalytic Dialogues* 1: 29–51.

Aron, L. (1992). Interpretation as expression of the analyst's subjectivity. *Psychoanalytic Dialogues* 2: 475–507.

Aron, L. (1996). *A meeting of minds: Mutuality in psychoanalysis.* Hillsdale, NJ: The Analytic Press.

Benjamin, J. (1998). *Shadow of the other: Intersubjectivity and gender in psychoanalysis.* New York: Routledge.

Benjamin, J. (2002). The mysteries of repetition and repair. Presented at Relational Analysts at Work: Sense & Sensibility, New York, January 19.

Black, M. (2002). Enactment: Analytic musings on energy, language, and personal growth. Presented at Relational Analysts at Work: Sense & Sensibility, New York, January 20.

Bollas, C. (1987). *The shadow of the object: Psychoanalysis of the unthought known*. New York: Columbia University Press.

Bridges, N. (1993). Clinical dilemmas: Therapists treating therapists. *American Journal of Orthopsychiatry* 63(91): 34–44.

Bridges, N. (1994). Meaning and management of attraction: Neglected aspects of psychotherapy training and practice. *Journal of Psychotherapy* 31: 424–433.

Bridges, N. (1995). Managing erotic and loving feelings in therapeutic relationships: A model course. *Psychotherapy Practice and Research* 4: 329–339.

Bridges, N. (1998). Teaching psychiatric trainees to respond to sexual and loving feelings: The supervisory challenge. *Psychotherapy Practice and Research* 7: 217–226.

Bridges, N. (1999). Psychodynamic perspective on therapeutic boundaries: Creative clinical possibilities. *Journal of Psychotherapy Practice & Research* 8(4): 292–300.

Bridges, N. (2000). The role of supervision in managing intense affect and constructing boundaries in therapeutic relationships. *Journal of Sex Education and Treatment* 24(4): 218–225.

Bridges, N. (2001). Therapist self-disclosure: Expanding the comfort zone. *Journal of Psychotherapy* 38(1): 21–30.

Bromberg, P. M. (1991). On knowing one's patient's inside out. *Psychoanalytic Dialogues* 1(4): 399–422.

Bromberg, P. M. (1998). *Standing in the spaces: Essays on clinical process trauma & dissociation*. Hillsdale, NJ: The Analytic Press.

Brown, L. (1994). When the therapist is a woman: Exploring the dynamics of same-sex therapy abuse. Presented at The Third International Conference on Sexual Exploitation by Health Professionals, Psychotherapists, and Clergy, Toronto, Canada, October 13–15.

Carroll, R. (1997). In sickness and in health. In *Countertransference in Couples Therapy*, ed. M. Solomon and J. Siegel, 187–200. New York: W.W. Norton & Co.

Casement, P. J. (1982). Some pressures on the analyst for physical contact during the reliving of an early trauma. *International Review of Psychoanalysis* 9: 279–286.

Cooper, S. (1998a). Analyst subjectivity, analyst disclosure, and the aims of psychoanalysis. *Psychoanalytic Quarterly* 67: 379–406.

Cooper, S. (1998b). Countertransference disclosure and the conceptualization of analytic technique. *Psychoanalytic Quarterly* 67: 128–154.

Cooper, S. (2003). You say oedipal, I say postoedipal: A consideration of desire and hostility in the analytic relationship. *Psychoanalytic Dialogues* 13(1): 41–63.

Darwin, J. (1999). Leaps and bounds: Impasse and intersubjectivity. *Smith College Studies in Social Work* 69(2): 457–473.

Davies, J. M. (1994a). Love in the afternoon: A relational reconsideration of desire and dread in the countertransference. *Psychoanalytic Dialogues* 4: 153–170.

Davies, J. M. (1994b). Desire and dread in the analyst: Reply to Glen Gabbard's commentary on "Love in the afternoon." *Psychoanalytic Dialogues* 4: 503–508.

Davies, J. M. (1998). Between the disclosure and foreclosure of erotic transference-countertransference: Can psychoanalysis find a place for adult sexuality? *Psychoanalytic Dialogues* 8: 747–766.

Davies, J. M. (2000). Descending the therapeutic slopes: Slippery, slipperier, slipperiest. *Psychoanalytic Dialogues* 10(2): 219–229.

Davies, J. M. (2002). Whose bad objects are these anyway?: Repetition and our elusive love affair with evil. Presented at Relational Analysts at Work: Sense & Sensibility, New York, January 19.

Davies, J. M. (2003). Falling in love with love: Oedipal and postoedipal manifestations of idealization, mourning, and erotic masochism. *Psychoanalytic Dialogues* 13(1): 1–27.

Davies, J. M., and Frawley, M. (1994). *Treating the adult survivor of childhood sexual abuse: Psychoanalytic perspectives.* New York: Basic Books.

Ehrenberg, D. B. (1992). *The intimate edge.* New York: W.W. Norton.

Ehrenberg, D. B. (1995). Self-disclosure: Therapeutic tool or indulgence? *Contemporary Psychoanalysis* 31: 213–228.

Elise, D. (1991). When sexual and romantic feelings permeate the therapeutic relationship. In *Gays, Lesbians, and Their Therapists*, ed. C. Silverstein, 52–67. New York: W. W. Norton & Co.

Epstein, L. (1977). The therapeutic function of hate in the countertransference. *Contemporary Psychoanalysis* 13: 442–468.

Epstein, L. (1995). Self-disclosure and analytic space. *Contemporary Psychoanalysis* 31(2): 229–236.

Epstein, R. (1994). *Keeping boundaries.* Washington, D.C.: American Psychiatric Press.

Fishman, G. (1999). Too hot to handle: Containing and symbolizing erotic overstimulation in the realm of the transgressive and traumatic. Presented at Boston Psychoanalytic Institute & Society, November 20.

Fonagy, P. (1999). *The process of change and the change of processes: What can change in a "good analysis."* Keynote Address to the Spring Meeting of Division 39 of the American Psychological Association, New York, April 16.

Fonagy, P., (2001). *Attachment and psychoanalysis.* New York: Other Press.

Fonagy, P., and Target, M. (1998). Mentalization and the changing aims of child psychoanalysis. *Psychoanalytic Dialogues* 8: 87–114.

Fonagy, P., Gergely, G., Jurist, E., and Target, M. (2002). *Affect regulation, mentalization, and the development of the self.* New York: Other Press.

Foreman, S. A. (1996). The significance of turning passive into active in control mastery theory. *Psychotherapy Practice & Research* 5(2): 106–121.

Fosshage, J. (1994). Toward reconceptualizing transference: Theoretical and clinical considerations. *International Journal of Psycho-Analysis* 75: 265–280.

Fosshage, J. (2000). The meanings of touch in psychoanalysis: A time for reassessment. *Psychoanalytic Inquiry* 20(1): 21–43.

Frankel, J. (2002). Exploring Ferenzi's concept of identification with the aggressor: Its role in trauma, everyday life, and the therapeutic relationship. *Psychoanalytic Dialogues* 12(1): 101–139.

Freidlander, S., Dye, N., Costello, R., and Kobos, J. (1984). A developmental model for teaching and learning in psychotherapy supervision. *Psychotherapy* 21(2): 189–196.

Gabbard, G. O. (ed.) (1989). *Sexual exploitation in professional relationships.* Washington, DC: American Psychiatric Press.

Gabbard, G. O. (1991). Technical approaches to transference hate in the analysis of borderline patients. *International Journal of Psycho-Analysis* 72: 625–637.

Gabbard, G. O. (1993). Introduction to observations on transference-love: Further recommendations on the technique of psychoanalysis III, by Freud. Reprinted in the *Journal of Psychotherapy: Practice and Research* 2(2): 170–180.

Gabbard, G. O. (1994a). Sexual excitement and countertransference love in the analyst. *Journal of the American Psychoanalytic Association* 42: 1083–1135.

Gabbard, G. O. (1994b). A response to Davies (But not the last word). *Psychoanalytic Dialogues* 4: 509–510.

Gabbard, G. O. (1995). Countertransference: The emerging common ground. *International Journal of Psychoanalysis* 76: 475–485.

Gabbard, G. O. (1996). *Love and hate in the analytic setting.* Northvale, NJ: Aronson.

Gabbard, G. O. (2000). Consultation from the consultant's perspective. *Psychoanalytic Dialogues* 10(2): 209–218.

Gabbard, G. O., and Lester, E. P. (1995). *Boundaries and boundary violations in psychoanalysis.* New York: Basic Books.

Gelb, P. (1982). The experience of nonerotic contact in traditional psychotherapy: A critical investigation of the taboo against touch. *Dissertation Abstracts* 43: 248B.

Goldstein, E. (1994). Self-disclosure in treatment: What therapists do and don't talk about. *Clinical Social Work Journal* 22(4): 417–433.

Goldstein, E. (1997). To tell or not to tell: The disclosure of events in the therapist's life to the patient. *Clinical Social Work Journal* 25(1): 41–58.

Gorkin, M. (1987). *The uses of countertransference.* Northvale, NJ: Aronson.

Gutheil, T. G., and Gabbard, G. O. (1993). The concept of boundaries in clinical practice: Theoretical and risk-management dimensions. *American Journal Psychiatry* 150: 188–196.

Havens, L. (1986). *Making contact: Use of language in psychotherapy.* Cambridge: Harvard University Press.

Havens, L. (1989). *A safe place: Laying the groundwork of psychotherapy.* Cambridge: Harvard University Press.

Havens, L. (1993). *Coming to life: Reflections on the art of psychotherapy.* Cambridge: Harvard University Press.

Herman, J. L., Gartrell, N., Olarte, S., Feldstein, M., and Localio, R. (1987). Psychiatrist-patient sexual contact: Results of a national survey, 11: Psychiatrist's attitudes. *American Journal of Psychiatry* 144: 164–169.

Hoffman, I. (1983). The patient as interpreter of the analyst's experience. *Contemporary Psychoanalysis* 19: 389–422.

Hoffman, I. (1992a). Expressive participation and psychoanalytic discipline. *Contemporary Psychoanalysis* 28: 1–15.

Hoffman, I. (1992b). Some practical implications of a social-constructivist view of the psychoanalytic situation. *Psychoanalytic Dialogues* 2(3): 387–304.

Hoffman, I. (1994). Dialectical thinking and therapeutic action in the psychoanalytic process. *Psychoanalytic Quarterly* 63: 187–218.

Hoffman, I. (2002). Forging difference out of similarity: The multiplicity of corrective experience. Presented at Relational Analysts at Work: Sense & Sensibility, New York, January 19.

Horowitz, M. H. (2004). On revenge and masochism. Presented at Institute for Psychoanalytic Training and Research, New York, April 16.

Hutt, C., Scott, J., and King, M. (1983). A phenomenological study of super-visees' positive and negative experiences in supervision. *Psychotherapy: Theory, Research and Practice* 20(1): 118–122.

Jacobs, D. (1998). Father, can't you see I'm burning? Understanding the unusual in erotic life. Presented at Psychoanalysis and Sexuality: Reflections on an Old Love Affair, Boston, April 22.

Jacobs, D., David, R., and Meyer, D. J. (1995). *The supervisory encounter.* New Haven: Yale University Press.

Jacobs, T. (1991). On the question of self-disclosure by the analyst: Error or advance in technique? *Psychoanalytic Quarterly* 68: 159–183.

Jacobs, T. (2002). On unconscious communication and covert enactments: Some reflections on their role in the analytic situation. Presented at Relational Analysts at Work: Sense & Sensibility, New York, January 20.

Kernberg, O. F. (1992). *Aggression in personality disorders and perversions.* New Haven: Yale University Press.

Lakin, M. (1991). *Coping with ethical dilemmas in psychotherapy.* New York: Pergamon Press.

Lehrer, R. (1994). Some thoughts on self-disclosure and the danger-safety balance in the therapeutic relationship. *Psychoanalytic Dialogues* 4(3): 511–516.

Levenson, E. (1996). Aspects of self-revelation and self-disclosure. *Contemporary Psychoanalysis* 32(2): 237–248.

Lyons-Ruth, K. (1999). The two-person unconscious: Intersubjective dialogue, enactive relational representation, and the emergence of new forms of relational organization. *Psychoanalytic Inquiry* 19: 576–617.

Lyons-Ruth, K. (2000). "I sense that you sense that I sense . . . " Sander's recognition process and the specificity of relational moves in the psychotherapeutic setting. *Infant Mental Health Journal* 21: 85–98.

Lyons-Ruth, K. (2004). Enactive representation and the two-person unconscious. In L. Arons & A. Harris (eds.), *Relational Psychoanalysis, Vol. II.* Hillsdale, NJ: Analytic Press. In press.

Lyons-Ruth, K., Stern, D., Sander, L., Nahum, J., Harrison, A., Morgan, A., Bruschweiler-Stern, N., and Tronick, E. Z. (1998). Implicit relational knowing: Its role in development and psychoanalytic treatment. *Infant Mental Health Journal* 19: 282–289.

Maroda, K. (1991). *The power of countertransference.* New York: Wiley.

Maroda, K. (1999a). *Seduction, surrender, and transformation: Emotional engagement in the analytic process.* Hillsdale, NJ: Analytic Press.

Maroda, K. (1999b). Creating an intersubjective context for self-disclosure. *Smith College Studies in Social Work* 69(2): 475–489.

McLaughlin, J. (1991). Clinical and theoretical aspects of enactment. *Journal of the American Psychoanalytic Association* 39: 595–614.

McLaughlin, J. (1995). Touching limits in the analytic dyad. *Psychoanalytic Quarterly* 64: 433–465.

McLaughlin, J. (1996). Power, authority, and influence in the analytic dyad. *Psychoanalytic Quarterly* 65: 201–235.

McLaughlin, J. (2000). The problem and place of physical contact in analytic work: Some reflections on handholding in the analytic situation. *Psychoanalytic Inquiry* 20: 64–80.

Miller, J. B. (2000). Creative moments: Sources of change. Presented at Learning from Women, Harvard Medical School, Continuing Education Conference, April 29.

Mitchell, S. (1988). *Relational concepts in psychoanalysis: An integration.* Cambridge: Harvard University Press.

Mitchell, S. (1991). Contemporary perspectives on the self: Toward an integration. *Psychoanalytic Dialogue* 1: 121–147.

Mitchell, S. (1997). *Influence and autonomy in psychoanalysis.* Hillsdale, NJ: The Analytic Press.

Mitchell, S. (2000). *Relationality: From attachment to intersubjectivity.* Hillsdale, NJ: The Analytic Press.

Modell, A. (1990). Dilemmas of the therapeutic relationship. Presented at Essentials of Psychotherapy, Harvard Medical School, Continuing Education Conference, June 22.

Ogden, T. H. (1982). *Projective identification and psychotherapeutic technique.* New York: Jason Aronson.

Ogden, T. H. (1985). On potential space. *International Journal of Psycho-Analysis* 66: 129–141.

Ogden, T. H. (1994). The analytic third: Working with intersubjective clinical facts. *International Journal of Psycho-Analysis* 75: 3–19.

Orbach, S. (2000). *The impossibility of sex: Stories of the intimate relationship between therapist and patient.* New York: Scribner.

Peterson, M. R. (1992). *At personal risk: Boundary violations in professional-client relationships.* New York, W.W. Norton & Co.

Pizer, B. (1997). When the analyst is ill: Dimensions of self-disclosure. *The Psychoanalytic Quarterly* 66(3): 450–469.

Pizer, B. (1998). When the crunch is a (k)not: A crimp in relational dialogue. Presented at Paul L. Russell Psychotherapy Symposium Crisis and Repetition: The Crucibles of Emotional Growth, November 6.

Pizer, B. (2000). The therapist's routine consultations: A necessary window in the treatment frame. *Psychoanalytic Dialogues* 10(2): 197–207.

Pizer, B. (2003). When the crunch is a (k)not: A crimp in relational dialogue. *Psychoanalytic Dialogues* 13(2): 171–192.

Pizer, S. A. (1992). The negotiation of paradox in the analytic process. *Psychoanalytic Dialogues* 2(2): 215–240.

Pizer, S. A. (1996). The distributed self: Introduction to symposium on "The multiplicity of self and analytic technique." *Psychoanalytic Dialogues* 10(2): 197–207.

Pizer, S. A. (1998). Building bridges: The negotiation of paradox in psychoanalysis. Hillsdale, NJ: Analytic Press.

Pizer, S. A. (2000). The role of consultations in the prevention of boundary violations. *Psychoanalytic Dialogues* 10(2): 195–196.

Rauch, P. K., Muriel, A. C., and Cassam, E. (2002). When a parent has cancer: Who's looking after the children. *Journal Clinical Oncology* 20(21): 4399–4402.

Renik, O. (1991). Playing one's cards face up in analysis: An approach to the problem of self-disclosure. *Psychoanalytic Quarterly* 68: 521–539.

Renik, O. (1995). The ideal of the anonymous analyst and the problem. *The Psychoanalytic Quarterly* 62(3): 466–495.

Ringstrom, P. A. (2001). Cultivating the improvisational in psychoanalytic treatment. *Psychoanalytic Dialogues* 1(5): 727–754.

Ringstrom, P. A. (2003). A relational intersubjective approach to conjoint treatment. Presented at Massachusetts Institute of Psychoanalysis, October 4.

Robbins, B. (2000). Under attack: Devaluation and the challenge of tolerating the transference. *Journal of Psychotherapy Practice & Research* 9(3): 136–141.

Robiner, W. N. (1982). Role diffusion in the supervisory relationship. *Professional Psychology* 13(2): 258–267.

Rodolfa, E., Kitzow, M., Vohra, S., and Wilson, B. (1990). Training interns to respond to sexual dilemmas. *Professional Psychology Research & Practice* 21: 313–315.

Roman, B., and Kay, J. (1997). Residency education on the prevention of physician-patient sexual misconduct. *Academic Psychiatry* 21: 26–34.

Russell, P. (1976a). The theory of the crunch. Unpublished manuscript.

Russell, P. (1976b). The structure and function of paradox in the treatment process. Unpublished manuscript.

Russell, P. (1976c). Beyond the wish: Further thoughts on containment. Unpublished manuscript.

Russell, P. (1976d). The negotiation of affect. Unpublished manuscript.

Russell, P. (1976e). Emotional growth and crises of attachment. Unpublished manuscript.

Russell, P. (1983). Personal communications.

Sander, L. W. (2002). Thinking differently: Principles of process in living systems and the specificity of being known. *Psychoanalytic Dialogues* 12(1): 11–42.

Searles, H. F. (1965). Oedipal love in the countertransference. In *Collected papers on schizophrenia and related subjects*, ed. H. F. Searles, 284–303. New York: International Universities Press.

Slavin, J. H., Rahmani, M., and Pollock, P. (1998). Reality and danger in psychoanalytic treatment. *Psychoanalytic Quarterly* 67: 191–217.

Stern, D. N., Sander, L. W., Nahum, J. P., Harrison, A. M., Lyons-Ruth, K., Morgan, A. C., Bruschweiler-Stern, N., and Tronick, E. Z. (1998). Non-interpretative mechanisms in psychoanalytic therapy: The "something-more" than interpretation. *International Journal of Psychoanalysis* 79: 903–921.

Stern, S. (1994). Needed relationships and repeated relationships: An integrated relational perspective. *Psychoanalytic Dialogues* 4(3): 317–346.

Stern, S. (2002). The self as a relational structure: A dialogue with multiple-self theory. *Psychoanalytic Dialogues* 12(5): 693–714.

Stolorow, R., Atwood, G., and Brandchaft, B. (eds.) (1997). *The intersubjective perspective*. Northvale, NJ: Jason Aronson.

Stolorow, R. D., and Atwood, G. E. (1992). *Contexts of being: The intersubjective foundations of psychological life*. Hillsdale, NJ: The Analytic Press.

Strasburger, L. H., Jorgenson, L. M., and Sutherland, P. (1991). The prevention of psychotherapist sexual misconduct: Avoiding the slippery slope. *American Journal of Psychotherapy* 46: 545–555.

Tansey, M. (1994). Sexual attraction and phobic dread in the countertransference. *Psychoanalytic Dialogues* 4(2): 139–152.

Tansey, M., and Burke, W. (1989). *Understanding countertransference: From projective identification to empathy*. Hillsdale, NJ: The Analytic Press.

Tansey, M. J., and Burke, W. F. (1991). Countertransference disclosure and models of therapeutic action. *Contemporary Psychoanalysis* 27: 351–384.

Teicholz, J. G., and Kreigman, D. (eds.) (1998). *Trauma, repetition, and affect regulation: The work of Paul Russell*. New York: Other Press.

Thorbeck, J. (1992). The development of the psychodynamic psychotherapist in supervision. *Academic Psychiatry* 16(2): 72–82.

Tronick, E., Bruschweiler-Stern, N., Harrison, A., Lyons-Ruth, K., Morgan, A., Nahum, J., Sander, L., and Stern, D. (1998). Dyadically expanded states of consciousness and the process of therapeutic change. *Infant Mental Health Journal* 19: 290–299.

Waldinger, R. J. (1994). Boundary crossings and boundary violations: Thoughts on navigating a slippery slope. *Harvard Review of Psychiatry* 2: 225–227.

Wells, T. (1994). Therapist self-disclosure: Its effects on clients and the treatment relationship. *Smith College Studies in Social Work* 65: 22–41.

Wilkinson, S., and Gabbard, G. O. (1993). Therapeutic self-disclosure with borderline patients. *Journal of Psychotherapy Practice & Research* 2(4): 282–295.

Winnicott, D. (1958). Hate in the countertransference. In *Collected papers: Through paediatrics to psychoanalysis*, ed. D. W. Winnicott, 194–203. London: Tavistock Publications.

Wolitzer, M. (2000). Sitting up and lying down. In *Tales from the couch*, ed. J. Shinder, 94–101. New York: Harper Collins.

Ulman, K. H. (2001). Unwitting exposure of the therapist: Transferential and countertransferential dilemmas. *Journal of Psychotherapy Practice and Research* 10(1): 14–22.

INDEX